My 80s

Fun & Facts

by
Sarah Lewis

Red Rain

For all the My 80s listeners,

thank you for joining me on our journey
through the diversity of the decade's music.

Introduction

The My 80s Radio Show celebrated its first anniversary at Mad Wasp Radio with a special party show. Featuring a playlist chosen by guests who had previously appeared in the Favourite Five slot, it began with The Quick's "Rhythm of The Jungle", the choice of my first ever Favourite Five guest, Modern Romance's Andy Kyriacou, and culminated with Europe's "Final Countdown", as selected by Spear of Destiny's Kirk Brandon, a man who had made me giggle like a schoolgirl during our interview. The show was a wonderful celebration of a year of 80's entertainment and chat, not to mention some of the decade's best music, at the station with a sting in its tail.

My 80s Fun & Facts takes a look back at that year, detailing the show's track lists and Back On Track, Word Up, Favourite Five and Our Choon features. In addition to the facts about the show, there is a bit of fun in the form of puzzles, crosswords, word searches and pop quiz. I've even included an extra Monster Mash Up quiz especially for the readers of this book, so make sure you've got your pens, paper and whiteboards ready to answer another devilishly difficult compendium of clips!

Thank you for buying this book and for listening to the show. I'll catch up with you same time, same place …

Sarah x

Contents

Favourite Five

One thing which makes My 80s stand out from other 80's radio shows is the Favourite Five feature, in which guests choose and talk about their favourite songs of the decade. Choices do not need to have made the UK Top 40 and may be album tracks. This has meant a wide variety of songs have been selected and played in this section of the show. The guests and the choices they made during our first year on Mad Wasp Radio are listed below.

David Brewis   **Show 2** 14/09/2017
My favourite song of the entire Eighties in "Closest Thing to Heaven" so I could think of no one better to be my first Favourite Five guest, following the show's move to Mad Wasp, than The Kane Gang's guitarist and songwriter.

"Videotheque" by Dollar
"I'm In Love With A German Film Star" by The Passions
"It's A Love Thing" by The Whispers
"All Night Long" by Mary Jane Girls
"Friends" by Shalamar

Peter Coyle   **Show 3** 21/09/2017
The former frontman with The Lotus Eaters discussed his collaboration with Toyah Wilcox on the song "Nine Hours" when he made his choices.

"The Sensual World" by Kate Bush
"Biko" by Peter Gabriel
"Ashes To Ashes" by David Bowie
"Sign O' The Times" by Prince
"Girl On A Swing" by Andy Summers and Robert Fripp

Erkan Mustafa   **Show 4** 28/09/2017
Best known for his portrayal of Roland Browning in Grange Hill, the actor surprised many of the listeners with his depth of musical knowledge.

"Should I Stay or Should I Go" by The Clash
"Vienna" by Ultravox

"Our House" by Madness
"Shout To The Top" by The Style Council
"Promised Land" by Joe Smooth

Andy Overall   Show 5 05/10/2017
Blue Zoo's Andy O revealed his obsession with fungi, and his latest song 'Funganista', when he came on the show.

"I Will Follow" by U2
"A Promise" by Echo and The Bunnymen
"Fashion" by David Bowie
"Once In A Lifetime" by Talking Heads
"Where Is My Mind" by Pixies

Nik Kershaw   Show 6 12/10/2017
The multi-talented singer, songwriter and guitarist chose a track from the most popular album to feature in this slot to date, Talk Talk's "The Colour of Spring".

"The Word Girl" by Scritti Politti
"Shout" by Tears For Fears
"I Still Haven't Found What I'm Looking For" by U2
"Life's What You Make It" by Talk Talk
"Two Tribes" by Frankie Goes To Hollywood

Steve Blacknell   Show 7 19/10/2017
The fast-talking presenter and Europe's first video jockey relayed some wonderfully entertaining anecdotes about the Eighties when he selected his tracks.

"I Ran" by A Flock of Seagulls
"Red Skies" by The Fixx
"Stepping Out" by Joe Jackson
"Fugazi" by Marillion
"Mull Of Timperley" by Frank Sidebottom

David Nash   Show 8 26/10/2017
Urban street artist Gnasher brought us tracks which reflected both his growth as an artist and his love of hip hop and rap.

"White Lines (Don't Do It)" by Grandmaster Flash and Melle Mel
"I Feel For You" by Chaka Khan

"No Sleep 'Til Brooklyn" by Beastie Boys
"Rebel Without A Pause" by Public Enemy
"Your Love" by Frankie Knuckles

Helen McCookerybook   Show 9 02/11/2017

The founder member of Helen and The Horns and The Chefs was the first female guest to appear on Favourite Five, and eloquently relayed the music industry's treatment of women during the Eighties.

"The Drum is Everything" by Carmel
"Ice Cream Factory" by The Associates
"Walk Out To Winter" by Aztec Camera
"N.I.T.A." by Young Marble Giants
"Youth of Eglington" by Black Uhuru

Bobby McVay   Show 10 09/11/2017

The one-time member of Sweet Dreams took time out from filming the video for "Amen" by The Fizz to talk about his choices and his tendency to be accident prone.

"Roses" by Haywoode
"Wake Me Up Before You Go Go" by Wham!
"Sweet Freedom" by Michael McDonald
"Dancing Tight" by Phil Fearon and Galaxy
"Somebody Else's Guy" by Jocelyn Brown

Eddie Roxy   Show 11 16/11/2017

Originally the keyboard player for Department S, and now fronting the band, the singer spoke about the industry changes he had encountered during that time.

"Party Fears Two" by The Associates
"Christian" by China Crisis
"Pretty In Pink" by The Psychedelic Furs
"Not The Man I Used To Be" by Fine Young Cannibals
"She Bangs The Drums" by The Stone Roses

Mari Wilson   Show 12 23/11/2017

The queen of the beehives recalled nights at Camden Palace and over-the-top fashions when she took us through her track selection.

"Love Action" by The Human League

"Once In A Lifetime" by Talking Heads
"Sign O' The Times" by Prince
"I Don't Believe in You" by Talk Talk
"Relax" by Frankie Goes To Hollywood

Paula Ann Bland   Show 13   30/11/2018
She played Grange Hill's Claire Scott, and some of the actress's song choices were influenced by the fictional schoolgirl.

"She Sells Sanctuary" by The Cult
"Rio" by Duran Duran
"True" by Spandau Ballet
"99 Red Balloons" by Nena
"Take On Me" by A-ha

Tracie Young   Show 14   07/12/2017
Entering the music business at the tender age of 17, when she sang on The Jam's "Beat Surrender", the singer turned DJ had lots of behind-the-scenes snippets to tell us.

"Save It For Later" by The Beat
"Tribute" by The Pasadenas
"Touch And Go" by Any Trouble
"Madam Butterfly" by Malcolm McLaren
"I Can Dream About You" by Dan Hartman

Alan Read   Show 15   17/12/2017
Our Monster Mash Up quiz master was the first Favourite Five guest to appear on the show, following its move to Sunday evenings.

"Mirror In The Bathroom" by The Beat
"This Charming Man" by The Smiths
"Heaven" by The Psychedelic Furs
"Slave To The Rhythm" by Grace Jones
"Pop Life" by Prince

Tanya Raftery   Show 16   24/12/2017
The Christmas show gave one lucky listener the opportunity to choose their Favourite Five.

"Primitive Painters" by Felt
"Computer Love" by Kraftwerk
"Beat My Guest" by Adam And The Ant
"Debaser" by Pixies
"Mercy Street" by Peter Gabriel

John Bowen and Wayne Lee   Show 17 31/12/2017
The New Year's Eve show was a Liverpool special, and two Scousers I had known since we became Smash Hits penfriends in 1986 were my highly entertaining Favourite Five guests.

"Raintown" by Deacon Blue
"New Song" by Howard Jones
"Don't You Want Me" by The Human League
"This Woman's Work" by Kate Bush
"Edge of Heaven" by Wham!

Clive Jackson   Show 18 07/01/2018
The lead singer of Doctor & The Medics gave us a rocking start to 2018, with stories about Lemmy and song writing for The Damned.

"Killed By Death" by Motörhead
"Stranger on The Town" by The Damned
"Real Wild Child" by Iggy Pop
"Two Tribes" by Frankie Goes To Hollywood
"Do You Remember Rock 'n' Roll Radio" by The Ramones

Sarah Lewis   Show 19 14/01/2018

Having put my guests through the ordeal of choosing only five songs from our favourite decade, I thought it was only fair that I should do the same. Interviewing me about my choices was singer and song writer Owen Paul.

"Closest Thing To Heaven" by The Kane Gang
"Immaculate Fools" by Immaculate Fools
"My Favourite Waste of Time" by Owen Paul
"Street Tuff" by Double Trouble & The Rebel MC
"Visions In Blue" by Ultravox

Dave Barbarossa   Show 20   21/01/2018

The former drummer with Adam And The Ants and Bow Wow Wow chose some classic pop and took us back to a time when he was touring the States and clubbing in New York with Madonna.

"Never Too Much" by Luther Vandross
"You Spin Me Round (Like A Record)" by Dead or Alive
"Like A Virgin" by Madonna
"Mama Used To Say" by Junior
"Modern Love" by David Bowie

John Hammond   Show 21   28/01/2018

Following the success of the Christmas show, the end of January saw the first of our monthly Listener's Favourite Five. Guests also reveal what was the worst thing about the Eighties for them. My opening interviewee in this regular feature was someone I agreed with wholeheartedly, when he said the worst thing about the decade was its ending.

"Tunnel of Love" by Fun Boy Three
"Change" by Tears For Fears
"Valentine's Day" by ABC
"The Sun Always Shines On TV" by A-ha
"Sweet Love" by Anita Baker

Karel Fialka   Show 22   11/02/2018

The singer/song writer of the 1987 Top 10 hit single "Hey Matthew" spoke about his recent move from Malta to the Scottish Highlands, and his imminent new role as grandfather to Matthew's baby.

"The Great Curve" by Talking Heads
"Libertango" by Grace Jones
"Ashes To Ashes" by David Bowie
"Love Changes Everything" by Climie Fisher
"True Faith" by New Order

Gary Daly   Show 23   18/02/2018

The founding member of China Crisis entertained us with an insight into the Liverpool scene during the Eighties, band rivalries and touring with Paul Young.

"Wishing (If I Had A Photograph of You)" by A Flock of Seagulls
"Pale Shelter" by Tears For Fears

"Airwaves" by Thomas Dolby
"Brilliant Mind" by Furniture
"Messages" by Orchestral Manoeuvres in the Dark

Samantha Marcus   Show 24 25/02/2018

This listener revealed her worst thing about the Eighties was when she was run over as a child, but a silver lining appeared in the form of Darth Vader!

"Hysteria" by Def Leppard
"Touch The Fire" by Icehouse
"Should've Known Better" by Richard Marx
"Such A Shame" by Talk Talk
"I've Been Losing You" by A-ha

Max Splodge   Show 25 04/03/2018

The "Two Pints of Lager and A Packet of Crisps, Please" singer not only chatted about a more alternative Eighties but his ancestral links to Genghis Khan.

"Staring At The Rude Boys" by The Ruts
"Cry For Love" by Iggy Pop
"This Wheels On Fire" by Siouxsie & The Banshees
"68 Guns" by The Alarm
"Happy Talk" by Captain Sensible

Jenny Colgan   Show 26 11/03/2018

The award-winning author and 80's fan excitedly recalled her teenage years, plus her love of cooking, Paul Young and Dr. Who.

"Duel" by Propaganda
"Love Is A Battlefield" by Pat Benatar
"This Corrosion" by The Sisters of Mercy
"Tomb of Memories" by Paul Young
"Rattlesnakes" by Lloyd Cole & The Commotions

John Parr   Show 27 18/03/2018

With soundtracks to St. Elmo's Fire and Three Men And A Baby to his credit, and collaborations with artists including Tina Turner and Foreigner, the Grammy-nominated musician had plenty to discuss during his time on the feature.

"Boys of Summer" by Don Henley
"Rosanna" by Toto
"The Way It Is" by Bruce Hornsby & The Range
"Jump" by Van Halen   Jump
"Hard Habit To Break" by Chicago

Daniel Leisey   **Show 28** 25/03/2018
We crossed the pond to Pennsylvania for this listener's choices. Not only did he provide a different perspective on the decade's music, but he also enlightened us on the subject of 'valley girl' lingo.

"Don't Change" by INXS
"Twilight Zone" by Golden Earring
"Words" by Missing Persons
"Never Say Never" by Romeo Void
"Why Me?" by Planet P

Grahame Skinner   **Show 29** 01/04/2018
Hipsway's lead singer spoke of his love of cats and otters when he chose his tracks, and how an emotional connection with music can be hugely influential in how a song is remembered.

"The Killing Moon" by Echo & The Bunnymen
"The Message" by Grand Master Flash & the Furious Five
"Happiness Is Easy" by Talk Talk
"Party Fears 2" by The Associates
"Tinseltown In The Rain" by The Blue Nile

Michael Grant   **Show 30** 08/04/2018
Musical Youth's smiley keyboard player talked tattoos and twins during his interview, letting us in on his not so rock and roll lifestyle since he became a father.

"Don't Worry, Be Happy" by Bobby Mcferrin
"Livin' On A Prayer" by Bon Jovi
"When Doves Cry" by Prince
"Every Breath You Take" by The Police
"Buffalo Soldier" by Bob Marley

Owen Paul

My birthday show interviewer returned to Favourite Five to choose his own tracks, which included a performance by his brother, Brian McGee.

"Where The Streets Have No Name" by U2
"Slave To The Rhythm" by Grace Jones
"Themes From Great Cities" by Simple Minds
"A Different Corner" by George Michael
"Duel" by Propaganda

Sarah Jane Morris
Show 32 22/04/2018

One of the handful of guests who pushed the boundaries on what constitutes an 80's track, the singer with the unmistakable dark, smoky voice told us about *that* Top of The Pops performance with The Communards, and chatting with Peter Gabriel.

"Come On Eileen" by Dexys Midnight Runners
"Slow Love" by Prince
"My Ever Changing Moods" by The Style Council
"The Piano Has Been Drinking" by Tom Waits
"Don't Give Up" by Peter Gabriel and Kate Bush

Claire Glavin
Show 33 29/04/2018

A long and painful stay in hospital was the worst thing about the Eighties for this listener but, unable to do much except listen to music, it did help to deepen her love for the decade's releases.

"Nobody's Fool" (12" version) by Haircut 100
"I'll House You" by Jungle Brothers
"Drowning in Berlin" by The Mobiles
"Looking for Clues" by Robert Palmer
"Love Is In Control" by Donna Summer

Graeme Clark
Show 34 06/05/2018

Wet Wet Wet's former bass player spoke extensively about how some of the best tracks of the decade did not always receive the commercial success they deserved.

"Drive" by The Cars
"Cloudbusting" by Kate Bush
"Rapture" by Blondie

"Tempted" by Squeeze
"Free Fallin'" by Tom Petty

Kirk Brandon   Show 35 20/05/2018
Spear of Destiny's lead singer recalled his days of clubbing at The Blitz, and explained how the controlled society of today contrasts greatly with the freedom and individuality we enjoyed in the Eighties.

"Police and Thieves" by Junior Murvin
"West One (Shine On Me)" by The Ruts
"Das Modell" by Kraftwerk
"You're Wondering Now" by The Specials
"The Final Countdown" by Europe

Jaki Graham   Show 36 03/06/2018
The Brummie singer spoke of her friendship and touring with former Dooby Brother Michael McDonald, and performing with Cliff Richard, alongside Percy Sledge and James Ingram.

"Call Me" by Go West
"Sweet Freedom" by Michael McDonald
"Easy Lover" by Phillip Bailey and Phil Collins
"I Knew You Were Waiting" by Aretha Franklin and George Michael
"Owner of A Lonely Heart" by Yes

James Parks   Show 37 17/06/2018
When this listener said he thought the worst thing about the Eighties was Live Aid, because it killed music, I had to get him on the show to explain his somewhat controversial opinion.

"Story of The Blues" by Wah!
"Nothing Looks The Same In The Light" by Wham!
"Smalltown Boy" by Bronski Beat
"Shelter From The Rain" by All About Eve
"Nine While Nine" by The Sisters of Mercy

Chris Amoo   Show 38 01/07/2018
The Real Thing's frontman spoke candidly about losing his brother Eddy earlier in the year, and the first time performing without him on stage.

"Lovely Day" by Bill Withers
"Children of The Ghetto" by Philip Bailey
"After The Love Has Gone" by Earth, Wind and Fire
"Let's Do It Again" by The Staple Sisters
"Love Won't Let Me Wait" by Luther Vandross

Denise Pearson   Show 39 15/07/2018

Five Star's lead singer told us about her forthcoming children's book and her aspiration to marry Lionel Ritchie when she appeared on the show.

"Alone" by Heart
"Dancing On The Ceiling" by Lionel Ritchie
"I Found Lovin'" by The Fatback Band
"The Voice" by John Farnham
"Black Velvet" by Alannah Myles

Russell Hastings   Show 40 29/07/2018

Song writing, interpreting lyrics and working with Paul Weller were just some of the areas covered when From The Jam's singer and guitarist talked about his selection of tracks.

"Life's What You Make It" by Talk Talk
"Headstart For Happiness" by The Style Council
"Somewhere In My Heart" by Aztec Camera
"Let's Dance" by David Bowie
"Waiting On A Friend" by The Rolling Stones

Simon Crowby   Show 41 12/08/2018

The BBC decommissioning Dr. Who in 1989 was the worst thing about the Eighties for the last listener, in our first year at Mad Wasp Radio, to choose his Favourite Five.

"Desdemona" by The Kids From Fame
"Safety Dance" by Men Without Hats
"Clouds Across The Moon" by The Rah Band
"Lean On Me" by Red Box
"Love On The Run" by The Human League

Favourite Five Archives   **Show 42** 26/08/18

With the show's first anniversary looming, we took a look back at some of the tracks played on the feature during the past year.

"The Word Girl" by Scritti Politti - from Show 6, chosen by Nik Kershaw.

"Messages" by OMD - from Show 23, chosen by Gary Daly

"West One (Shine On Me)" by The Ruts - from Show 35, chosen by Kirk Brandon.

"I Don't Believe In You" by Talk Talk - from Show 12, chosen by Mari Wilson.

"Madam Butterfly" by Malcolm McLaren - from Show 14, chosen by Tracie Young.

Note: There was no Favourite Five on Show 43.

Favourite Five Wordsearch No. 1

```
N  R  J  K  W  A  H  S  K  A  J  G  R  A  H  M  K  I  N
I  E  U  G  R  E  N  N  I  K  S  E  M  A  H  A  R  G  S
K  N  N  S  Y  D  S  X  N  P  K  I  R  B  Y  G  N  S  E
K  N  I  T  S  E  L  U  A  P  A  H  U  J  M  Y  O  D  E
E  G  O  Y  J  E  T  J  O  A  R  A  S  A  I  R  D  N  D
R  X  R  S  U  N  L  L  N  U  R  T  S  K  R  I  K  V  E
S  N  G  T  N  A  O  L  U  L  J  N  L  G  E  A  I  K  V
S  Y  I  O  I  V  H  G  H  A  O  G  F  R  B  D  C  N  A
W  S  S  C  M  K  N  F  X  A  H  S  O  D  R  Y  N  R  N
R  T  C  E  K  C  M  Y  K  N  S  X  X  N  A  R  R  A  U
A  O  O  D  E  I  A  D  I  N  Y  T  O  O  N  A  U  L  O
P  W  M  D  I  N  H  D  E  B  P  D  I  S  P  G  I  S  C
A  A  B  L  A  N  A  E  Y  L  N  S  R  N  U  J  O  C  A
U  H  E  R  N  E  R  O  X  A  S  C  H  D  G  E  M  J  I
L  U  C  U  N  R  G  I  R  N  B  O  M  N  D  S  B  U  R
A  O  U  S  B  S  I  B  I  D  J  M  B  R  A  K  O  N  Y
B  C  O  L  L  S  K  R  H  A  M  B  P  K  O  B  C  I  K
Y  L  A  D  Y  R  A  G  G  R  A  E  A  P  R  R  S  O  Y
A  G  R  A  I  H  J  N  K  H  M  W  R  S  N  I  R  G  D
L  A  Y  K  O  A  N  D  Y  W  A  H  S  R  E  K  K  I  N
D  N  R  I  A  C  U  O  K  H  A  S  T  I  G  N  O  D  A
```

Andy Kyriacou	Junior Giscombe
Eddie Roxy	Kirk Brandon
Gary Daly	Nick Van Eede
Grahame Skinner	Nik Kershaw
Jaki Graham	Paula Ann Bland
John Parr	Russell Hastings

Answers at back of book

Favourite Five Crossword

All the clues relate to songs and artists featured on Favourite Five

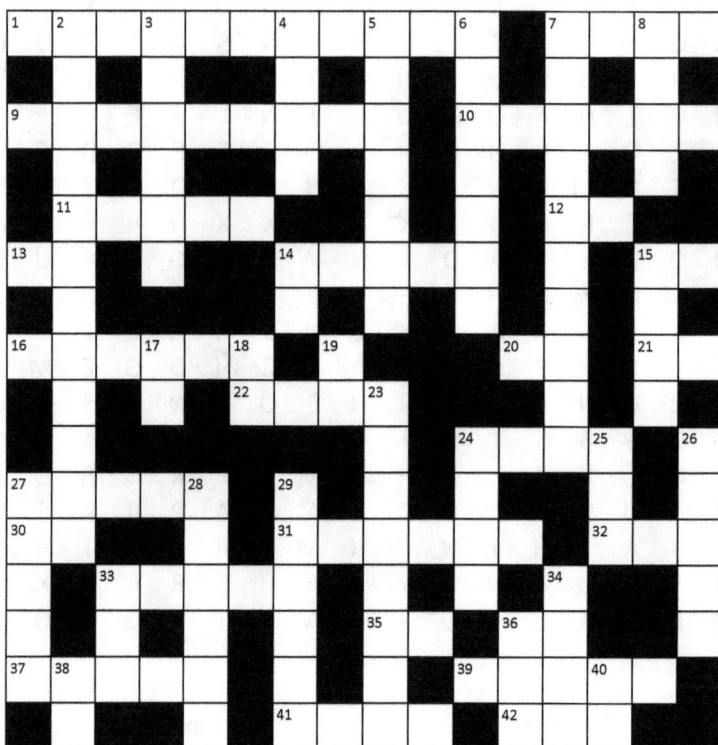

Across

1 & 10 across Album by 13 across (3,6,2,6)
7 Soft Cell's David (4)
9 See 2 down
10 See 1 across
11 Football team supported by 16 across, 27 across in short (5)
12 & 15 across, 15 down Pixies' song "Where __ __ ____" (2,2,4)
13 Initially they told us Life's What You Make It (1,1)
14 Mr Johnson came up in conversation with 21 across (5)
15 See 12 across
16 & 27 across This guest loves you when you sleep (6,5)
20 Initially this guest is politically correct (1,1)

14

21 Initially he sang "When A Heart Beats" (1,1)

22 Conservation for one of the bands chosen by Gary Daly? (1,1,1,1)

24 Ms Wilson chose a track from 1 across (4)

27 See 16 across

30 & 31 across, 25 down Second part of the question asked by The Clash (2,6,1,2)

31 See 30 across

32 Where Joe Jackson was stepping (3)

33 Did ABC shoot a poison one on Valentine's Day? (5)

35 Initially Imagination's lead singer (1,1)

36 Initially the first song choice of 24 across (1,1)

37 Does Denise Pearson want to hear Lionel say this? (5)

39 She does this to the Stone Roses' drums (5)

41 Max Splodge chose a track about 68 of these (4)

42 Jaki Graham's final choice was by this band (3)

Down

2 & 9 across The Style Council track chosen by 5 down (9,3,9)

3 Ancestral island of Andy Kyriacou (5)

4 This Paul was a guest on Show 31 (4)

5 From The Jam's Mr Hastings (7)

6 David Bowie track chosen by Andy Overall (7)

7 John Foxx track chosen by 7 across (7,3)

8 Bucks Fizz's one was make believe (4)

14 Initially Kirk Brandon chose this track by The Ruts (1,1)

15 See 12 across

17 Initially The Real Thing's frontman (1,1)

18 Regal initials of Department S' lead singer (1,1)

19 2 down features on the Café Bleu one (1,1)

23 Beastie Boys had no sleep until they got there (8)

24 Frank Sidebottom sang about one in Timperley (4)

25 See 30 across

26 Camera chosen by Helen McCookerybook (5)

27 Dennis Seaton and Michael Grant are musical (5)

28 & 29 down Andy Summers & Robert Fripp song chosen by 20 across (4,2,1,5)

29 See 28 down

33 David Brewis chose "___ Night Long" (3)

34 The Mary ____ Girls sang 33 down (4)

36 One of Jenny Colgan's choices was renowned for doing this with his hat (3)

38 Initially he was Grange Hill's Roland Browning (1,1)

40 Initially the lead singer of Hipsway

Answers at back of book

Favourite Five Wordsearch No. 2

```
K  A  R  L  D  E  A  K  L  A  I  F  L  E  R  A  K  A  N
I  F  E  E  E  N  I  S  L  D  A  V  I  D  B  M  A  L  L
A  L  R  E  L  H  C  T  A  D  K  R  A  L  C  U  C  M  L
A  K  F  E  P  E  A  R  B  L  Y  O  C  W  O  S  A  C  A
P  T  O  J  S  S  O  N  D  P  E  T  L  I  Y  T  Y  V  B
E  T  N  O  S  L  I  W  I  R  A  M  A  L  L  A  D  A  D
T  E  P  H  B  D  A  S  V  K  R  H  R  S  E  F  I  V  A
E  R  S  N  O  Y  N  O  A  A  E  E  K  O  N  A  J  E  N
N  K  L  E  E  E  R  N  D  L  E  L  E  N  O  C  O  N  N
A  A  I  L  K  L  J  E  E  J  E  E  R  N  S  M  L  O  N
G  F  W  I  L  S  O  N  K  H  B  L  D  C  D  A  G  S  Y
L  D  A  J  N  N  H  E  Y  O  N  Y  C  R  L  R  A  R  N
O  E  M  T  E  R  N  B  B  M  O  O  A  E  A  A  N  A  N
C  N  Y  Y  S  K  A  B  E  U  N  C  T  L  N  I  R  E  E
Y  I  B  A  C  U  Y  D  R  S  S  R  C  H  O  R  K  P  J
N  I  B  Y  V  M  M  Y  O  T  D  E  F  M  D  A  D  E  C
N  S  O  B  C  A  W  N  K  N  L  T  I  B  N  M  A  S  O
E  E  B  V  R  R  I  I  A  A  A  E  K  A  A  E  T  I  L
J  P  A  E  R  S  O  N  N  K  I  P  A  L  I  E  L  N  G
O  Y  C  L  R  K  S  O  F  F  R  E  R  L  K  L  E  E  A
N  S  D  L  A  N  O  D  N  A  I  E  J  O  H  N  R  D  H
```

Bobby McVay	Ian Donaldson
Clark Datchler	Jenny Colgan
David Ball	Karel Fialka
Denise Pearson	Leee John
Erkan Mustafa	Mari Wilson
Helen McCookerybook	Peter Coyle

Answers at back of book

Back On Track

There were some great songs in the Eighties which were never released as a single. That's where the 'Back On Track' feature comes in. Every week, a listener chooses a track from any album that was released during our favourite decade. The only condition that has to be met is that their choice was never released as a single in the UK. Below are the Back On Track choices played during the past year.

Show 1 09/09/2017
"Reeling" by Then Jerico from "The Big Area"

Show 2 14/09/2017
"Mystic Rhythms" by Rush from "Power Windows"

Show 3 21/09/2017
"Love Is A Contact Sport" by Whitney Houston from "Whitney"

Show 4 28/09/2017
"If You Were Here" by The Thompson Twins from "Quick Step & Side Kick"

Show 5 05/10/2017
"WXJL" Tonight by Human League from "Travelogue"

Show 6 12/10/2017
"Hold Me Now" by The Adventures from "The Sea of Love"

Show 7 19/10/2017
"Heartbeat" by Wham! from "Make It Big"

Show 8 26/10/2017
"S.O.S." by Go West from "Go West"

Show 9 02/11/2017
"Living A Boy's Adventure Tale" by A-ha from "Hunting High And Low"

Show 11 16/11/2017
"Is It Love" by Milli Vanilli from "All or Nothing"

Show 12 23/11/2017
"Tread Water" by De La Soul from "Three Feet High And Rising"

Show 13 30/11/2017
"Talk To Me" by The Outfield from "Play Deep"

Show 14 07/12/2017
"Making History" by Adam And The Ants from "Kings of The Wild Frontier"

Show 15 17/12/2017
"Paradise" by New Order from "Brotherhood"

Show 17 31/12/2017
"Find A Reason" by River City People from "Say Something Good"

Show 18 07/01/2018
"Shopping" by Pet Shop Boys from "Actually"

Show 19 14/01/2018
"Wallflower" by Peter Gabriel from "Security"

Show 20 21/01/2018
"Got It Made" by Holly Johnson from "Blast"

Show 21 28/01/2018
"The Wrong Road" by The Go-Betweens from "Liberty Belle And The Black Diamond Express"

Show 22 11/02/2018
"Christie Lee" by Billy Joel from "An Innocent Man"

Show 23 18/02/2018
"A Man of Great Promise" by The Style Council from "Our Favourite Shop"

Show 24 25/02/2018
"Heaven Only Knows" by ELO from "Balance of Power"

Show 25 04/03/2018
"Nirvana" by The Cult from "Love"

Show 26 11/03/2018
"Don't Mess With Me" by Karyn White from "Karyn White"

Show 27 18/03/2018
"The Wedding List" by Kate Bush from "Never For Ever"

Show 28 25/03/2018
"Who's Gonna Catch You" by Mel & Kim from "F.L.M."

Show 29 01/04/2018
"Human's Lib" by Howard Jones (title track)

Show 30 08/04/2018
"More Than A Party" by Depeche Mode from "Construction Time Again"

Show 31 15/04/2018
"When The Angels" by Prefab Sprout from "Two Wheels Good"

Show 32 22/04/2018
"Sweet Thing" by Yazoo from "You And Me Both"

Show 33 29/04/2018
"Where's The Party" by Madonna from "True Blue"

Show 34 06/05/2018
"The Kingdom" by Icehouse from "Man of Colours"

Show 35 20/05/2018
"An Elegant Chaos" by Julian Cope from "World Shut Your Mouth"

Show 36 03/06/2018
"Cold Dark and Yesterday" by Hall & Oates from "Big Bam Boom"

Show 37 17/06/2018
"You Broke My Heart In 17 Places" by Tracey Ullman (title track)

Show 38 01/07/2018
"A Matter of Feeling" by Duran Duran from "Notorious"

Show 39 15/07/2018
"The Dive" by Culture Club from "Waking Up With The House On Fire"

Show 40 29/07/2018
"A Ray of Sunshine" by Wham! from "Fantastic"

Show 41 12/08/2018
"Transformer Man" by Neil Young from "Trans"

Show 42 26/08/18
"Code of Love" by Spandau Ballet from "True"

Note: There was no Back On Track feature on shows 10, 16 and 43.

Back On Track Anagrams

Unravel the anagrams to find tracks and artists which have been played on the Back On Track feature.

1.   Anglo Hates Acne by Nicola Jupe

2.   Radar Tweet by Leo Aldus

3.   Pensively Restitches by Cheri Musty

4.   Hermione Hell Kit by Dead Manhattans

5.   Demon Howl by Trusted Heaven

6.   Gwenneth Heals by Turbo Frappes

7.   Bluish Man by Jason Whored

8.   Fannies Road by Clive Pete Priory

9.   Falwell Row by Piglet Bearer

10. Geri Len by John Recite

11. Geek Held Town by Joann Jackets

12. Crested Germany by Edee Chomped

13. Elite Riches by Jill Boyle

14. Mrs Sum Accountant by Ahmed Dent

15. Glistened Width by Shut Beak

Answers at back of book

Back On Track Wordsearch

```
A  G  O  T  Y  T  R  A  P  E  H  T  S  E  R  E  H  W  T
M  I  S  W  R  R  G  R  E  A  T  P  R  O  M  I  S  A  A
A  T  I  H  T  A  H  E  A  R  T  B  A  T  E  B  M  S  L
N  D  T  E  O  S  P  A  R  T  Y  E  M  G  D  A  K  H  K
O  A  T  R  W  W  W  A  H  E  L  O  V  E  N  E  L  O  T
F  M  O  E  T  Y  M  E  R  R  O  T  H  O  M  M  A  W  M
G  E  G  S  R  T  A  E  T  T  V  E  F  R  L  O  T  M  O
R  T  I  T  H  E  P  S  N  I  Y  G  I  V  G  T  N  A  E
P  R  O  M  I  S  S  E  W  V  R  A  N  A  T  T  I  D  K
O  L  O  G  E  W  D  G  I  E  R  A  E  H  T  H  R  S  K
M  E  V  N  M  E  O  O  A  D  E  T  W  R  T  I  V  E  I
T  N  I  I  O  E  M  T  K  A  T  T  P  A  Y  N  A  W  N
A  G  I  H  T  T  P  M  I  M  O  R  T  E  E  G  N  H  G
E  K  L  A  T  R  O  O  N  T  M  E  R  H  W  N  A  E  M
B  I  N  G  O  M  D  D  G  I  E  A  H  T  I  A  W  R  O
T  N  A  M  N  I  I  N  I  T  A  L  K  A  R  N  S  E  D
R  A  I  W  I  A  A  V  R  O  I  N  I  E  I  N  G  K  O
A  S  H  O  K  N  M  O  D  G  N  I  K  B  N  V  N  I  M
E  I  M  E  G  A  L  O  V  E  I  T  S  I  R  A  I  N  I
H  I  T  E  M  O  T  K  L  A  T  H  I  N  G  N  D  O  M
G  R  E  A  T  M  A  N  I  S  E  P  R  O  M  A  N  A  R
```

A Man of Great Promise	Nirvana
Got It Made	Show Me
Heartbeat	Sweet Thing
Is It Love	Talk To Me
Kingdom	Where's The Party

Answers at back of book

Monster Mash Up

Preceded every show by the one-track-warning alarm, Monster Mash Up features ten clips of songs from the Eighties for the listener to identify. This teasing test of music knowledge is presented by our quiz meister extraordinaire, Alan Read, who chooses one of the tracks to be played in full after he has revealed the answers. Scan the QR code to find an extra Monster Mash Up we have put together, especially for readers of this book. This has been 'hidden' on my website. As another little treat, Alan has also devised this pop quiz.

1. "Between The Lines" and "Silk and Steel" are 80's albums by which group?

2. What was Debbie Gibson's debut British hit single?

3. John Keeble is the drummer with which band?

4. How many people attended the London Live Aid concert: 72,000, 82,000 or 92,000?

5. Which politician appears in the Tracey Ullman video for "My Guy"?

6. "Im Nin Alu" was a hit for which Israeli singer?

7. What was the name of Frankie Goes To Hollywood's second and final studio album?

8. Which song by The Smiths took Sandie Shaw back into the Top 20 in 1984, after a 15-year absence?

9. The 1980 No.1 single "Call Me" features in which movie starring Richard Gere?

10. What was the best-selling album in the UK during the 1980s?

11. "I'm not leaving now honey, not a chance" is a line from which 80's hit?

12. Which 80's hit songs by ABC and Madonna share a title?

13. What was the first single released from George Michael's "Faith" album?

14. Pseudo Echo had their only UK hit in 1987 with a cover of which song?

15. "Together We Are Beautiful" and "Use It Up and Wear It Out" reached No.1 in which year?

16. Paul McCartney and Michael Jackson had two hit duets in the Eighties. What were they?

17. Which group had Top 5 hits with "London Nights" and "Requiem"?

18. "Hello" and "Running With The Night" were taken from which Lionel Ritchie album?

19. Who sang with Donny Hathaway on the 1980 Top 3 hit "Back Together Again"?

20. How many winners of the Eurovision Song Contest reached No.1 in the UK during the Eighties?

Answers at back of book

Our Choon

Not long after we began the Monster Mash Up feature on the show, there were some comments made about the vocal similarity of our very own Alan Read and legendary Radio 1 DJ, Simon Bates. Memories of many a tearful time spent listening to Batesy regaling us with tales of heartbreak, over the theme to Romeo and Juliet, in his Our Tune feature, came flooding back to me, and an idea began to form. What if we could create a spoof version, using the storyline of a popular movie from the Eighties?

After much thought and a few attempts at writing the script, this is the one I finally settled on for the first Our Choon. Alan's delivery of the script, and subsequent Our Choons, can be found in the shows stated below, which have been archived on my Mixcloud page: www.mixcloud.com/sarah-lewis7/

Our Choon No. 1 Show 10, 9th November 2017

We're going back to the summer of '84 for today's Our Choon. Our tale of fighting against the odds for both love and for what is right comes from a young man who wishes to remain anonymous, so we'll just call him Mac for now.

An only child, Mac grew up in Chicago - a city he loved. Athletic and with a love for music, Mac would spend countless hours playing sport, dancing or simply driving around with his favourite sounds blasting from the speakers of his VW Beetle. However, Mac's life was turned upside down when his father died while Mac was still in high school.

Struggling to cope as a single parent, and with mounting financial worries, Mac's mother decided they should relocate to the Midwest, so they moved in with her sister, brother-in-law and two young nieces, Amy and Sarah. Although far from an ideal situation, Mac was happy to see his mother smiling again, and endeavoured to adapt to his surroundings.

One of the first things he did was join his mother and his extended family on their Sunday morning visit to church. During the service, his attention was drawn to a girl who bore a striking resemblance to the annoying, whiny actress who had flatly sung "It's Gonna Be A Long Night" in the television series Fame. Sitting in the pew next to her friend Rusty, the girl displayed a total disdain for the sanctity of the building she was in by painting her nails a bright shade of red, as the reverend delivered his sermon. Mac was immediately attracted to her.

Later on, after the service had finished, Mac was introduced to the reverend, and was surprised to learn that the rebellious nail-painter was in fact the minister's daughter. His interest further piqued, Mac was undeterred when he discovered the girl already had a boyfriend called Chuck. It was a discovery he made shortly after starting at his new high school.

Mac's first day at Bomont High was fraught with the daunting experiences of being the new kid in a strange town. When everybody stared at him as he pulled up into the school's car park, Mac wondered if he should have dressed down instead of looking like David Bowie, as his mother had commented. However, upon befriending the lovably simple country boy, Willard Hewitt, Mac discovered that the town of Bomont had banned the playing of popular music, as well as dancing. It was the loud music coming from his car's speakers that had attracted all the stares.

As Mac struggled to come to terms with the potential loss of two of his loves in life, his attraction for the reverend's daughter, biblically named Ariel, strengthened. It was something that didn't go unnoticed by Chuck, who challenged his love rival to a game of chicken, driving tractors. Despite the fact that Mac had never driven a tractor before, he was victorious and forced Chuck to jump off his tractor, and land in a water-filled ditch. Unknown to all who witnessed the farmland duel, Mac's victory was down to the fact that he had been unable to jump from his tractor, as his shoelace had become entangled with the pedals.

Ariel, who had been holding out for a hero, was so impressed with Mac's handling of his equipment that she dumped Chuck and began dating Mac, or to give him his full name, Ren McCormack.

The pair's first night out together was a double date with Willard and Rusty, which saw the four teenagers drive over the state line so they could go dancing. During the evening, Ren made two important discoveries. The first was that Willard couldn't dance. The second was that music and dance had been banned in Bomont following the death of Ariel's older brother, in a car crash five years earlier, when he was returning from a night of dancing. It explained why Ariel's father was so set against Ren's idea to hold a senior prom.

Undeterred by the challenges in front of him, Ren set about teaching Willard how to dance, even engaging the help of his young cousins, who helped Willard get rid of his two left feet and total lack of rhythm. The reverend and the anti-dancing laws proved more of a problem.

At a town council meeting, Ren raised the subject of abolishing those laws, citing passages from the bible, as directed by Ariel, to support his proposal. It was all to no avail, as the council voted against the idea. However, all was not lost because the boss of the grain mill where Ren had a part-time job, offered his premises for the prom. Just outside of Bomont's town limits, the grain mill was the ideal location for the dance.

When the reverend asked his congregation to pray for all of those who were going to the prom, and even bought Ariel a corsage to wear for the evening, it seemed like all was right in the world ... and it would have been if Chuck and his pals hadn't turned up outside the grain mill. They set upon Willard, as he and Rusty arrived at the dance.

Outnumbered five to one, Willard looked set to take a beating. That was until Ren appeared and helped his best friend tackle the cowardly quintet. Very quickly, Ren and Willard saw off their adversaries, much to the delight of their partners. They celebrated by dancing the night away.

Ren stayed devoted to Ariel, at least until thanksgiving 1987, when he was glimpsed in New York racing Steve Martin for a yellow cab before Steve journeyed across America with John Candy.

This is the song that reminds Ren of his time with Ariel and their hard-fought-for prom night.

["Footloose" by Kenny Loggins plays]

*****

The My 80s listeners seemed to enjoy our take on this classic radio feature, so I wrote another Our Choon, which went out on the Christmas show.

Our Choon No. 2 Show 16, 24th December 2017

Our festive tale of the trials of love takes us back to 1988. This was the year when Christmas became even more memorable and special for Holly.

Estranged from her husband for six months, Holly juggled raising their two children with her job as director of corporate affairs. It was a position that saw her still at work early in the evening on Christmas Eve.

However, the fact that she had only to spend a little while longer with her colleagues at their office Christmas party, before returning home, kept her smiling. That and the knowledge that her husband would be spending Christmas with them, in an attempt to reconcile their marriage. Holly had no idea of the extraordinary efforts he would make to ensure the success of their reunion.

During the course of Holly's office party, trouble broke out when a group of aggressive gate-crashers forced entry into the festivities. Her boss, Joe, left the party, took the trouble-makers into another room, and tried to placate them. It was something he failed to achieve and paid for with his life.

Holly's husband, John, witnessed the incident, having arrived at the office to meet his wife shortly beforehand. Moonlighting from his job as a policeman, John realised the severity of the situation, and the huge danger Holly and her colleagues were in.

His initial attempts to inform the authorities of events fell on deaf ears, so John was forced to take matters into his own hands. John had always said he would walk on broken glass for Holly, and this particular Christmas Eve he did just that.

As violence from the interlopers increased, John fought back in a number of ways, including throwing explosives down a lift shaft, abseiling off the roof of the office block suspended only by a fire hose, and engaging in hand-to-hand combat with a murderous German named Karl.

John's finest moment however, came when he rescued Holly from the evil clutches of the assailants' leader, saving her from being dragged out of a high-rise window, to certain death. It was also a time when John realised that Max Bygraves had not told the truth, and you most certainly did not need Hans.

If anything, the opposite was true. For since John's seasonal heroics in 1988, many people have felt it's not really Christmas until you've seen Hans Gruber fall from the top of the Nakatomi Building.

Although Holly disappeared from the limelight, John continues to fight evil to this very day. Old habits die hard.

That special Christmas Eve is remembered by Holly whenever she hears this next song. Merry Christmas and yippee kay yay My 80s listeners!

["Christmas In Hollis" by Run-D.M.C. plays]

*****

It seemed only right to include an Our Choon in the Mad Wasp Radio first anniversary show. However, with listeners eager to identify the movie upon which I had based the script, I had to come up with something a little bit different if they weren't to guess it in the first few sentences. The answer lay in combining an 80's No. 1 single and its video.

Our Choon No. 3   Show 43, 9th September 2018

We begin tonight's Our Choon by going back to the early Eighties, when a young man named Tom found himself unwittingly in the middle of a love triangle.

Somewhat geeky in appearance, with a love for science and transmitting, Tom writes that the whole experience left him feeling frightened and restless.

"At times," says Tom "I scare myself thinking about what could have happened. It got to a point where I was so stressed with nervous energy, I became agitated, hyperactive even."

Tom recalls an evening shortly after he became engaged to his long-suffering girlfriend Judy. "Long-suffering" explains Tom because she had for some time tolerated his ongoing friendship with Babs, a slightly eccentric girl with a love of all things oriental, especially the Japanese martial art, Kendo.

Bearing more than a passing resemblance facially to bubbly, blonde Judy, raven-haired Babs could not have been more different in personality.

Whereas Judy was outgoing and fun, Babs was incredibly serious and intense. This was never more apparent than when Tom and Judy arrived at a party Babs was throwing to celebrate her birthday.

An eclectic bunch of partygoers, even by 1981 standards, were gathered. Although many guests looked as though they had wandered out of The Blitz nightclub, some were so lifeless and devoid of personality, they could have been mannequins.

However, the most disturbing thing about the night was when Babs broke down sobbing uncontrollably, before singing about her woes to her guests.

Tom says it was definitely a night to remember, for all the wrong reasons, and this is the song that takes him back to that extraordinary evening.

["It's My Party" by Dave Stewart and Barbra Gaskin plays]

Word Up

One of the challenges of putting together each My 80s show is sorting through the requests submitted by listeners. Selecting only one track each show for the Word Up feature, in which listeners choose songs that include a particular word in the lyrics or title, is often incredibly difficult because so many good suggestions are put forward. Here are the songs that have appeared on the feature during our first year at Mad Wasp Radio (Word Up is in capital letters).

Show 1 07/09/2017
"Let's Go CRAZY" by Prince

Show 2 14/09/2017
"The SECOND Summer of Love" by Danny Wilson

Show 3 21/09/2017
"Chance" by Big Country (RAIN)

Show 4 28/09/2017
"So COLD The Night" by The Communards

Show 5 05/10/2017
"POOR Man's Son" by Survivor

Show 6 12/10/2017
"Will You" by Hazel O'Connor (DRINK)

Show 7 19/10/2017
"KEEP Moving" by Madness

Show 8 26/10/2017
"Don't be AFRAID of the Dark" by The Robert Cray Band

Show 9 02/11/2017
"FIRE Woman" by The Cult

Show 10 09/11/2017
"A Good YEAR For The Roses" by Elvis Costello

Show 11 16/11/2017
"U Got The Look" by Prince (BOOK)

Show 12 23/11/2017
"All of My HEART" by ABC

Show 13 30/11/2017
"There Is A LIGHT That Never Goes Out" by The Smiths

Show 14 07/12/2017
"A WINTER's Tale" by David Essex

Show 15 17/12/2017
"A QUESTION of Lust" by Depeche Mode

Show 18 07/01/2018
"NEW Moon on Monday" by Duran Duran

Show 19 14/01/2018
"Missionary Man" by Eurythmics (BORN)

Show 20 21/01/2018
"Hazy Shade of Winter" by The Bangles (TIME)

Show 21 28/01/2018
"WHITE Boy" by Culture Club

Show 22 11/02/2018
"(Keep FEELING) Fascination" by The Human League

Show 23 18/02/2018
"Sgt. ROCK (Is Going To Help Me)" by XTC

Show 24 25/02/2018
"BIG In Japan" by Alphaville

Show 25 04/03/2018
"DREAMtime" by Hall & Oates

Show 26 11/03/2018
"Rapture" by Blondie (DOOR)

Show 27 18/03/2018
"NEVER Never" by The Assembly

Show 28 25/03/2018
"Blue Hat For A Blue DAY" by Nick Heyward

Show 29 01/04/2018
"FRIENDs Will Be Friends" by Queen

Show 30 08/04/2018
"In Your CAR" by The Cool Notes

Show 31 15/04/2018
"I Don't WANT Your Love" by Duran Duran

Show 32 22/04/2018
"EYES Without A Face" by Billy Idol

Show 33 29/04/2018
"UNDER Cover of The Night" by The Rolling Stones

Show 34 06/05/2018
"DOWN on The Street" by Shakatak

Show 35 20/05/2018
"BREAK My Stride" by Matthew Wilder

Show 36 03/06/2018
"Hey MUSIC Lover!" by S'Express

Show 37 17/06/2018
"Talking in Your SLEEP" by Bucks Fizz

Show 38 01/07/2018
"Computer GAME" by Yellow Magic Orchestra

Show 39 15/07/2018
"HEAT of the Moment" by Asia

Show 40 29/07/2018
"BOYS (Summertime Love)" by Sabrina

Show 41 12/08/2018
"Don't Dream It's OVER" by Crowded House

Show 42 26/08/18
"Can I PLAY With Madness" by Iron Maiden

Show 43 09/09/18
"FIRST We Take Manhattan" by Leonard Cohen

Note: There was no Word Up feature on shows 16 and 17

Word Up Anagrams

Unravel the anagrams to find tracks and artists which have been played on the Word Up feature.

1. Clothed Hosting by Chrome Dustman

2. Admits Flying Wench by Bodily Lil

3. Chooses Furled Movement by Lindon Yawns

4. Abroad Kindhearted Toff by Barty Cornbread

5. Denote Northwest by Ask Katha

6. Cher Hotted Unforgiven by Hollering Stetson

7. Ever Vernen by Bessy Therma

8. Be With Yo by Blue Curl Cut

9. Aidan Froths Wheezy by Basel Ghent

10. Latin Sweater by Devised Sax

11. Peru Rat by Ben Idol

12. Jab Paining by Lilah Pavel

13. Smiley Voucher by Press Sex

14. Emma Tried by Adena Shallot

15. Dreary Roofage Soothes by Covets Lollies

Answers at back of book

Word Up Wordsearch

```
A  Y  O  N  B  R  E  A  K  M  Y  T  R  I  S  E  D  F  I
L  B  O  M  R  K  O  O  L  E  H  T  T  O  G  U  A  E  R
L  N  M  N  B  I  T  T  R  A  E  H  F  I  R  Y  E  W
O  E  A  A  O  H  S  E  G  A  A  L  L  M  F  E  M  M  O
F  W  T  M  Y  W  T  R  A  C  R  U  O  Y  N  I  N  A  M
M  M  R  O  Y  I  R  P  M  O  C  G  O  E  E  W  O  G  B
Y  O  A  W  S  R  D  U  E  I  L  S  K  I  S  S  I  R  N
H  O  E  E  W  G  A  T  T  L  E  W  G  O  E  H  E  E  A
W  N  W  R  E  A  P  N  C  M  S  E  O  N  E  A  R  T  M
H  O  E  I  E  M  C  O  O  S  W  E  T  A  K  H  T  U  O
I  N  N  F  T  E  M  S  M  I  E  T  U  M  S  E  S  P  W
T  M  E  N  E  P  A  N  P  R  S  E  Y  R  W  A  M  M  F
B  O  Y  A  S  M  I  L  U  T  R  S  T  Y  E  R  I  O  R
U  N  A  F  T  I  R  Y  T  E  T  T  I  A  N  T  L  C  E
G  D  M  I  S  S  I  O  N  R  Y  S  A  M  E  A  E  A  I
O  A  O  R  M  S  N  A  I  W  O  M  N  A  T  L  O  R  H
T  Y  W  E  L  I  O  D  R  F  U  I  Y  P  U  L  E  H  T
T  M  O  O  N  O  E  Y  C  A  R  L  C  O  M  F  K  O  T
H  C  O  M  P  T  E  R  Y  O  B  E  T  I  H  W  G  O  O
E  R  E  T  U  S  N  E  W  M  O  N  D  A  Y  M  O  L  G
K  S  W  E  T  E  T  R  A  E  H  Y  M  F  O  L  L  A  U
```

All of My Heart	Missionary Man
Break My Stride	New Moon on Monday
Computer Game	Sweetest Smile
Fire Woman	U Got The Look
In Your Car	White Boy

Answers at back of book

My 80s Wordsearch

```
M  F  U  O  R  D  P  Q  U  E  S  T  F  I  V  E  S  R  O
O  A  O  D  E  T  E  U  W  A  S  P  R  E  Q  U  P  D  W
N  V  P  U  H  S  A  M  R  E  T  S  N  O  M  S  E  Q  U
S  U  O  O  M  I  P  A  D  U  O  L  S  C  I  A  C  C  R
T  P  H  L  O  X  L  C  U  D  G  U  E  T  X  R  A  T  E
C  R  K  C  A  R  T  N  O  K  C  A  B  M  H  A  L  S  S
K  A  A  X  W  A  S  M  A  D  W  A  A  O  X  E  G  U  E
B  T  R  I  F  R  T  Q  U  I  Z  P  S  N  T  V  B  E  Q
A  C  K  M  I  A  E  R  E  S  M  S  S  S  R  I  A  R  S
C  H  A  R  A  S  V  T  S  A  S  A  I  T  A  F  C  R  V
K  N  A  M  S  L  W  O  S  T  R  F  S  R  C  E  K  T  I
K  O  S  H  S  P  E  C  I  A  L  G  U  E  S  T  O  N  F
C  T  M  W  P  A  C  K  H  U  M  V  K  M  T  I  L  A  T
A  R  O  A  U  O  R  L  X  I  R  Z  C  A  S  R  E  C  I
W  X  N  L  D  W  E  A  O  L  C  I  I  S  E  U  W  K  X
A  I  S  C  W  W  O  R  D  U  P  T  T  U  U  O  W  I  R
S  M  E  C  I  L  A  H  L  E  W  F  S  P  Q  V  O  S  U
P  P  T  S  P  E  C  S  R  I  S  I  M  H  E  A  R  A  O
S  G  T  H  W  V  L  U  P  U  P  V  Z  I  R  F  D  R  V
E  S  R  A  M  I  O  N  S  T  R  E  U  X  S  A  W  H  A
U  Q  E  R  A  T  S  M  Z  I  U  Q  X  C  L  O  U  D  F
```

Back On Track	Quiz Master
Favourite Five	Requests
Mad Wasp	Sarah Lewis
Mixcloud	Special Guest
Monster Mash Up	Word Up

Answers at back of book

My 80s Playlists

Rarely does a week go past without me being asked if there is a list of the tracks that have been played on the show. Up until now, the answer has always been 'no'. However, I'm a great believer in giving people what they want (just check out the beginning of Show 15), so here are all the tracks I've played during My80s' first year on Mad Wasp Radio.

Track   Artist

Show 1

Track	Artist
Henry The Wasp	The Highliners
I Say Nothing	Voice of The Beehive
Shock The Monkey	Peter Gabriel
Carnation	The Jam
I've Been In Love Before	Cutting Crew
Life's What You Make It	Talk Talk
Leaving Me Now	Level 42
Could You Be Loved	Bob Marley
War Baby	Tom Robinson
Caterpillar	The Cure
Reeling	Then Jerico
(We Don't Need This) Fascist Groove Thang	Heaven 17
Torch	Soft Cell
First We Take Manhattan	Jennifer Warnes
Pearl In The Shell	Howard Jones
Shipbuilding	Elvis Costello
Let's Go Crazy	Prince
Never Too Much	Luther Vandross
Mistake No. 3	Culture Club
Maniac	Michael Sembello
Rat Race	The Specials
Dave	Boomtown Rats
Destination Unknown	Missing Persons
Spread A Little Happiness	Sting

Show 2

Track	Artist
I've Been Losing You	A-ha
Born To Me My Baby	Bon Jovi
German Girl	The Lotus Eaters
Forest Fire	Lloyd Cole & The Commotions
Sweet Thing	Yazoo

Closest Thing To Heaven	The Kane Gang
Videotheque	Dollar
I'm In Love With A German Film Star	The Passions
Male Stripper	Man II Man Meets Man Parrish
The Second Summer Of Love	Danny Wilson
More, More, More	Carmel
In Your Room	The Bangles
You Don't Own Me	The Blow Monkeys
Life On Your Own	Human League
It's A Love Thing	The Whispers
All Night Long	Mary Jane Girls
Years From Now	Dr Hook
The Medicine Song	Stephanie Mills
Motormania	Roman Holliday
Friends	Shalamar
When Your Dream Is Broken	David Brewis
Mystic Rhythms	Rush
In The Country	The Farmer's Boys

Show 3

Dance Little Sister	Terence Trent D'Arby
Tesla Girls	OMD
Burn It Up	The Beatmasters and PP Arnold
First Picture Of You	The Lotus Eaters
The Sensual World	Kate Bush
Biko	Peter Gabriel
Bird Of Paradise	Snowy White
The Taste Of Your Tears	King
Cruel Circus	The Colour Field
Love Is A Contact Sport	Whitney Houston
Ashes To Ashes	David Bowie
Sign O' The Times	Prince
(I Love You) When You Sleep	Tracie
Sinful	Pete Wylie
Maybe Tomorrow	The Chords
Electric Blue	Icehouse
Homely Girl	UB40
Walking In The Sunshine	Bad Manners
The Flyer	Saga
Girl On A Swing	Andy Summers and Robert Fripp
Nine Hours	Toyah and Peter

Chance	Big Country
Jeanette	The Beat
Out Of Reach	Vice Squad
Hide & Seek	Howard Jones

Show 4

Hi Ho Silver	Jim Diamond
Kiss This Thing Goodbye	Del Amitri
Nothing Means Nothing	Immaculate Fools
School Daze	W.A.S.P.
Should I Stay Or Should I Go	The Clash
Vienna	Ultravox
She Means Nothing To Me	Phil Everly & Cliff Richard
If You Were Here	The Thompson Twins
No Myth	Michael Penn
Deutscher Girls	Adam And The Ants
Ball & Chain	XTC
Our House	Madness
Shout To The Top	The Style Council
You Take My Breath Away	H2O
Dreamtime	Darryl Hall
The Circus	Erasure
Hand Held In Black And White	Dollar
Promised Land	Joe Smooth
Fairplay	Soul II Soul
So Cold The Night	The Communards
Driving Away From Home	It's Immaterial
Labelled With Love	Squeeze
C30 C60 C90 Go	Bow Wow Wow
Love Comes Quickly	Pet Shop Boys
Your Latest Trick	Dire Straits

Show 5

Free Fallin'	Tom Petty
Beethoven (Love To Listen To)	Eurythmics
The Whisper	The Selecter
Love Moves In Strange Ways	Blue Zoo
I Will Follow	U2
A Promise	Echo & The Bunnymen
Can't Be Sure	The Sundays
WXJL Tonight	Human League
Somebody Else's Guy	Jocelyn Brown
Can't Stop The Music	The Village People
Fashion	David Bowie

Once In A Lifetime	Talking Heads
Dance	The Lambrettas
Run For Your Life	Bucks Fizz
Another Place And Time	Donna Summer
Heaven	Psychedelic Furs
Ticker Tape Parade	Ian Donaldson
Love On The Rocks	Neil Diamond
Poor Man's Son	Survivor
Where Is My Mind	The Pixies
Funganista	Blue Zoo
Human Racing	Nik Kershaw
Sleepwalk	Ultravox
Cell 151	Steve Hackett
There There My Dear	Dexys Midnight Runners

Show 6

Boy In The Bubble	Paul Simon
Lay Your Hands On Me	Thompson Twins
Night Games	Graham Bonnet
When A Heart Beats	Nik Kershaw
The Word Girl	Scritti Politti
Shout	Tears For Fears
Come Live With Me	Heaven 17
Satisfied	Richard Marx
Missing	Terry, Blair & Anouchka
Will You	Hazel O'Connor
I Still Haven't Found What I'm Looking For	U2
Life's What You Make It	Talk Talk
WFL (Wrote For Luck)	Happy Mondays
Overkill	Men At Work
Levi Stubbs Tears	Billy Bragg
Sound Of Confusion	Secret Affair
Out Here On My Own	Irene Cara
Windpower	Thomas Dolby
Each And Every One	Everything But The Girl
Two Tribes	Frankie Goes To Hollywood
Hold Me Now	The Adventures
Severina	The Mission
Talk of The Town	The Pretenders
No Mercy	The Stranglers
Innocent Man	Billy Joel

Show 7

Riders On The Storm	Annabel Lamb

Everybody Have Fun Tonight	Wang Chung
Be True To Yourself	Big Sound Authority
Video	Jeff Lynne
I Ran	A Flock Of Seagulls
Red Skies	The Fixx
Heaven (Must Be There)	Eurogliders
Rock Hard	Suzi Quatro
Come Back	The Mighty Wah!
Heartbeat	Wham!
This Boy Loves The Sun	David Austin
Back In The High Life Again	Steve Winwood
So Good To Be Back Home Again	The Tourists
Alone Again Or	The Damned
Julie Ocean	The Undertones
Stepping Out	Joe Jackson
Fugazi	Marillion
Mull Of Timperley	Frank Sidebottom
Lovesong	The Cure
It Started With A Kiss	Hot Chocolate
You Don't Want Me Anymore	Steel Breeze
Funeral Pyre	The Jam
Keep Moving	Madness
Cat People	David Bowie
Blister In The Sun	Violent Femmes

Show 8

America	Neil Diamond
Those First Impressions	The Associates
Is It A Dream	Classix Nouveaux
The Thin Wall	Ultravox
White Lines	Grandmaster Flash and Melle Mel
I Feel For You	Chaka Khan
Graceland	The Bible
Love Like Blood	Killing Joke
Do Nothing	The Specials
Don't Be Afraid Of The Dark	Robert Cray Band
No Sleep 'Til Brooklyn	Beastie Boys
Rebel Without A Pause	Public Enemy
Parisienne Walkways	Thin Lizzy
Just Like Honey	The Jesus and Mary Chain
Generals and Majors	XTC
Wired For Sound	Cliff Richard
It's Your Night	James Ingram
S.O.S.	Go West

Your Love	Frankie Knuckles
I Love The Way You Love Me	Karyn White
Somewhere In The World There Is A Cowboy Smiling	Blue Zoo
When All's Well	Everything But The Girl
Stop	Sam Brown

Show 9

Dog Eat Dog	Adam And The Ants
Mated	Jaki Graham and David Grant
Cat Among The Pigeons	Bros
Thrush	The Chefs
The Drum Is Everything	Carmel
Ice Cream Factory	The Associates
Invitation	Tracie Young
It's You, Only You	Lene Lovich
We Take Mystery (To Bed)	Gary Numan
Fire Woman	The Cult
Walk Out To Winter	Aztec Camera
N.I.T.A.	Young Marble Giants
The Real Thing	Jellybean ft. Steven Dante
Waves	Blancmange
So Here I Am	UB40
I'll Tumble For Ya	Culture Club
It Couldn't Happen Here	Pet Shop Boys
Some People	Belouis Some
Youth of Eglington	Black Uhuru
The Sea	Helen McCookerybook
Sounds Like A Melody	Alphaville
I Don't Think That Man Should Sleep Alone	Ray Parker Jnr
Living A Boy's Adventure Tale	A-Ha
Fall In	Adam And The Ants

Show 10

Walls Come Tumbling Down	The Style Council
Watching The Wildlife	Frankie Goes To Hollywood
Nobody's Diary	Yazoo
I'm Never Giving Up	Sweet Dreams
Roses	Haywoode
Wake Me Up Before You Go Go	Wham!
The Lunatics Have Taken Over The Asylum	Fun Boy Three
Last Night A DJ Saved My Life	Indeep
Wide Boy	Nik Kershaw
A Good Year For The Roses	Elvis Costello

Sweet Freedom	Michael McDonald
Dancing Tight	Galaxy
One For The Mockingbird	Cutting Crew
For The Very First Time	Robin Beck
Every Day	Jason Donovan
The Sensual World	Kate Bush
Cry Me A River	Mari Wilson
Just Say No	Grange Hill Cast
Somebody Else's Guy	Jocelyn Brown
Amen	The Fizz
Hold Me Now	Johnny Logan
One Step Further	Bardo
What	Soft Cell
Dear Prudence	Siouxsie and The Banshees
Footloose	Kenny Loggins

Show 11

I'll Be Satisfied	Shakin' Stevens
Stay Out Of My Life	Five Star
Dancing With Tears In My Eyes	Ultravox
Is Vic There?	Department S
The Associates	Party Fears Two
Christian	China Crisis
Oh Yeah (There's A Band Playing On The Radio)	Roxy Music
Is It Love	Milli Vanilli
Invincible	Pat Benatar
Ziggy Stardust	Bauhaus
Pretty In Pink	Psychedelic Furs
Not The Man I Used To Be	Fine Young Cannibals
Johnny and Mary	Robert Palmer
Rockit	Herbie Hancock
Rock The Night	Europe
Still On Fire	Aztec Camera
The Lady In My Life	Michael Jackson
The Sun And The Rain	Madness
U Got The Look	Prince
She Bangs The Drums	Stone Roses
When All Is Said And All Is Done	Department S
Masterpiece	Gazebo
Sharing The Night Together	Dr Hook
Kissing A Fool	George Michael

Show 12

Living In America	James Brown
The Smile and the Kiss	Bonk
Twist of Fate	Olivia Newton John
Just What I Always Wanted	Mari Wilson
Love Action	The Human League
Once In A Lifetime	Talking Heads
Blind Vision	Blancmange
Edge Of A Broken Heart	Vixen
Dinner With Gershwin	Donna Summer
Tread Water	De La Soul
Sign O' The Times	Prince
I Don't Believe in You	Talk Talk
Tragic Comedy	Immaculate Fools
Modern Day Delilah	Van Stephenson
Hourglass	Squeeze
Even The Trees	All That Jazz
I Just Grew Tired	Black
Forgotten Town	The Christians
All Of My Heart	ABC
Relax	Frankie Goes To Hollywood
Don't Talk To Strangers	Rick Springfield
Here Comes The Man	Boom Boom Room
Mad Eyed Screamer	The Creatures

Show 13

P.Y.T.	Michael Jackson
Messages	OMD
Ku Ku Kurama	Paul Young
Clare	Fairground Attraction
She Sells Sanctuary	The Cult
Rio	Duran Duran
Broken Wings	Mr Mister
You Make My Dreams	Hall & Oates
The Promise	When In Rome
Talk To Me	The Outfield
True	Spandau Ballet
99 Red Balloons	Nena
Man Child	Neneh Cherry
I Just Wanna	
(Spend Some Time With You)	Alton Edwards
Wait	Robert Howard and
	Kym Mazelle
Head Over Heels	Tears For Fears

There'll Be Sad Songs	Billy Ocean
Club Country	The Associates
Jane Says	Jane's Addiction
There Is A Light That Never Goes Out	The Smiths
Take On Me	A-ha
Just Who Is The 5 O'Clock Hero	The Jam
Saturday Love	Cherelle & Alexander O'Neal
Let Me Go	Heaven 17

Show 14

End Of The Line	Traveling Wilburys
Someone's Looking At You	Boomtown Rats
People Hold On	Coldcut ft. Lisa Stansfield
The House That Jack Built	Tracie
Save It For Later	The Beat
Tribute	The Pasadenas
Bound To Be	The Dream Academy
We're Having All The Fun	Fun Boy Three
Der Kommisar	After The Fire
A Winter's Tale	David Essex
Touch And Go	Any Trouble
Madam Butterfly	Malcolm McLaren
Love Is All That Matters	The Human League
Could Have Told You So	Halo James
7 Teen	The Regents
Making History	Adam And The Ants
20 Seconds To Comply	Silver Bullet
I Can Dream About You	Dan Hartman
A Night in New York	Elbow Bones and the Racketeers
Roadblock	Stock, Aitken & Waterman
Keeping The Dream Alive	Freiheit
Freak	Bruce Foxton
Bridge To Your Heart	Wax

Show 15

Give The People What They Want	The Kinks
State of Shock	Mick Jagger and Michael Jackson
I Wanna Be A Winner	Brown Sauce
Answer Me	The Silencers
Mirror In The Bathroom	The Beat
This Charming Man	The Smiths
Pillar To Post	Aztec Camera

Why Can't I Be You?	The Cure
I Think It's Love	Jermaine Jackson
Question of Lust	Depeche Mode
Gina	Stray Cats
Heaven	Psychedelic Furs
Slave To The Rhythm	Grace Jones
Let It All Blow	Dazz Band
Hold The Heart	Big Country
Ooh To Be Ah	Kajagoogoo
Why Worry	Dire Straits
Walking Down Your Street	The Bangles
Skin Trade	Duran Duran
Paradise	New Order
Pop Life	Prince
Ed's Funky Diner	It's Immaterial
Listen To The Radio (Atmospherics)	Tom Robinson and Crew
Ain't Nothing Going On But The Rent	Gwen Guthrie
Visions of China	Japan

Show 16

Winter Wonderland	Eurythmics
Stars Over 45	Chas 'n' Dave
One Christmas Catalogue	Captain Sensible
Beat My Guest	Adam And The Ants
Primitive Painters	Felt
I Saw Mommy Kissing Santa Claus	John Cougar Mellencamp
December Will Be Magic Again	Kate Bush
Blue Christmas	Shakin' Stevens
She Won't Be Home	Erasure
Do You Hear What I Hear?	The Carpenters
Computer Love	Kraftwerk
Debaser	Pixies
Christmas On Riverside Drive	August Darnell
Christmas In Hollis	Run-D.M.C.
Mele Kalikimaka	Bing Crosby and The Andrew Sisters
Feliz Navidad	Boney M
Hard Candy Christmas	Dolly Parton
San Damiano (Heart And Soul)	Sal Solo
Christmas Wrapping	The Waitresses
Thank God It's Christmas	Queen
Mercy Street	Peter Gabriel
A Spaceman Came Travelling	Chris De Burgh
Fairytale Of New York	The Pogues & Kirsty MacColl

Show 17

Going Down To Liverpool	The Bangles
(Just Like) Starting Over	John Lennon
Valotte	Julian Lennon
There She Goes	The La's
Raintown	Deacon Blue
New Song	Howard Jones
Can't Get By Without You	The Real Thing
Love Is A Wonderful Colour	Icicle Works
Born To Run	Frankie Goes To Hollywood
Find A Reason	River City People
Don't You Want Me	Human League
This Woman's Work	Kate Bush
I Will Be With You	T'Pau
Best Kept Secret	China Crisis
Veronica	Elvis Costello
Driving Away From Home	It's Immaterial
The First Picture of You	The Lotus Eaters
Come Back	The Mighty Wah!
Treason (It's Just A Story)	The Teardrop Explodes
Edge of Heaven	Wham!
Burn	Doctor and The Medics
The More You Live The More You Love	A Flock Of Seagulls
Sweetest Smile	Black
Happy New Year	Abba

Show 18

Danger Zone	Kenny Loggins
He Ain't No Competition	Brother Beyond
Hands Off She's Mine	The Beat
Spirit In The Sky	Doctor and The Medics
Killed By Death	Motörhead
Stranger On The Town	The Damned
President Am I	Slow Children
Shopping	Pet Shop Boys
Ordinary Angel	Hue and Cry
Friends	Amii Stewart
Real Wild Child	Iggy Pop
Two Tribes	Frankie Goes To Hollywood
I Wonder If You Take Me Home	Lisa Lisa and Cult Jam with Full Force
Can't Stop Running	Space Monkey
She Talks In Stereo	Gary Myrick and The Figures
Eye Know	De La Soul

New Beginning (Mamba Seyra)	Bucks Fizz
Is That Love?	Squeeze
Do You Remember Rock 'n' Roll Radio	The Ramones
Just Like Paradise	David Lee Roth
New Moon on Monday	Duran Duran
Run Away	10cc
Stories of Johnny	Marc Almond
Come Hell or Waters High	Dee C Lee

Show 19

Grandpa's Party	Monie Love
I Hate Myself For Loving You	Joan Jett & The Blackhearts
Flaming Sword	The Care
Closest Thing To Heaven	The Kane Gang
Immaculate Fools	Immaculate Fools
More Songs About Chocolate And Girls	The Undertones
Nasty Girl	Vanity 6
Sleeping Bag	ZZ Top
Missionary Man	Eurythmics
My Favourite Waste of Time	Owen Paul
Street Tuff	Double Trouble and The Rebel MC

The Sun Rising	The Beloved
State of The Nation	Industry
Irene	The Photos
You Keep It All In	The Beautiful South
This House	Big Sound Authority
Be Near Me	ABC
Mirror Mirror	Dollar
Visions In Blue	Ultravox
Amazing	Owen Paul
Wallflower	Peter Gabriel
Captain of Her Heart	Double
Banana Republic	Boomtown Rats
When Am I Going To Make A Living?	Sade

Show 20

Johnny B. Goode	Marty McFly With The Starlighters
Bankrobber	The Clash
Burnin' For You	Blue Oyster Cult
C30, C60, C90, Go	Bow Wow Wow
Never Too Much	Luther Vandross
You Spin Me Round (Like A Record)	Dead or Alive

Body Work	Hot Streak
Got It Made	Holly Johnson
Vienna Calling	Falco
I Want To Be Your Property	Blue Mercedes
Like A Virgin	Madonna
Mama Used To Say	Junior
Heart of Gold	Johnny Hates Jazz
The Queen & The Soldier	Suzanne Vega
European Son	Japan
Torture	King
Read 'Em And Weep	Meat Loaf
I Heard A Rumour	Bananarama
Flesh For Fantasy	Billy Idol
Modern Love	David Bowie
I'm Not The Man I Used To Be	Fine Young Cannibals
Hazy Shade of Winter	The Bangles
Such A Shame	Talk Talk
Midnight Blue	Louise Tucker
The Shop Assistants	The Train From Kansas City
Deutscher Girls	Adam And The Ants

Show 21

Jennifer She Said	Lloyd Cole & The Commotions
Since Yesterday	Strawberry Switchblade
Tunnel of Love	Fun Boy Three
Change	Tears For Fears
Three Minute Hero	The Selecter
White Boy	Culture Club
Imagination	Belouis Some
She Wants To Dance With Me	Rick Astley
Valentine's Day	ABC
The Sun Always Shines On TV	A-ha
Disenchanted	The Communards
Ever So Lonely	Monsoon
Goodbye Girl	Go West
Are You Ready To Be Heartbroken?	Sandie Shaw
Cover Me	Bruce Springsteen
Ever Fallen In Love	Fine Young Cannibals
Sweet Love	Anita Baker
Credit Card Baby	Wham!
The Wrong Road	The Go-Betweens
She Makes My Day	Robert Palmer
Fantastic Life	The Fall

Don't Look Any Further | Dennis Edwards and
Seidah Garrett

Show 22

Nelson Mandela	Special AKA
Revolution Baby	Transvision Vamp
Shadow Of Love	The Damned
Hey Matthew	Karel Fialka
The Great Curve	Talking Heads
Libertango	Grace Jones
Sweet Sanity	Hurrah!
Christie Lee	Billy Joel
Angel Pale	Ian Donaldson
Ashes To Ashes	David Bowie
Love Changes Everything	Climie Fisher
Get Lucky	Jermaine Stewart
I Walk The Earth	Voice of The Beehive
Violently	Hue and Cry
Big Area	Then Jerico
Tinder	Hipsway
All of My Heart	ABC
True Faith	New Order
The Goodbye Look	Donald Fagen
(Keep Feeling) Fascination	Human League
She's In Parties	Bauhaus
When Love Breaks Down	Prefab Sprout
This Is Not A Love Song	PIL

Show 23

Pretty In Pink	Psychedelic Furs
Don't Waste My Time	Paul Hardcastle ft. Carol Kenyon
Oh Sheila	Ready For The World
Black Man Ray	China Crisis
Wishing (If I Had A Photograph of You)	A Flock of Seagulls
Pale Shelter	Tears for Fears
Sister of Mercy	Thompson Twins
A Man of Great Promise	The Style Council
Your Daddy Don't Know	Toronto
Out of Touch	Hall & Oates
Airwaves	Thomas Dolby
Brilliant Mind	Furniture
Underpass	John Foxx
Got To Get	Rob 'n' Raz ft. Leila K
Samson and Delilah	Bad Manners

The Big Sky	Kate Bush
Zoom	Fat Larry's Band
Let's Go Together	Change
Messages	OMD
Lawnchairs	Our Daughter's Wedding
Sgt. Rock (Is Going To Help Me)	XTC
The Chinese Way	Level 42

Show 24

Where Were You Hiding When The Storm Broke	The Alarm
Southern Freeez	Freeez
Never Give Up On A Good Thing	George Benson
Hysteria	Def Leppard
Touch The Fire	Icehouse
The Boy With The Thorn In His Side	The Smiths
Big In Japan	Alphaville
Hot Shot	Herman Brood and His Wild Romance

You'll Never Know	Hi Gloss
Behind The Groove	Teena Marie
Should've Known Better	Richard Marx
Such A Shame	Talk Talk
Down Town	One 2 Many
There's The Girl	Heart
Don't Get Me Wrong	Pretenders
Grey Day	Madness
(I Love You) When You Sleep	Tracie
Seven Seas	Echo & The Bunnymen
I've Been Losing You	A-ha
Crockett's Theme	Jan Hammer
Heaven Only Knows	ELO
Out With Her	The Blow Monkeys
Don't Let me Down Gently	The Wonder Stuff
People Have The Power	Patti Smith
Toy Soldiers	Martika

Show 25

Shirley	Shakin' Stevens
New Toy	Lene Lovich
Stupid Questions	New Model Army

| Two Pints Of Lager and a Packet of Crisps, Please | Splodgenessabounds |

Staring At The Rude Boys	The Ruts
Cry For Love	Iggy Pop
Pop Goes the World	Men Without Hats
Dreamtime	Darryl Hall
My World	Secret Affair
The Breaks	Kurtis Blow
This Wheels On Fire	Siouxsie and The Banshees
68 Guns	The Alarm
Life On Your Own	Human League
What I Am	Edie Brickell
Tears On The Telephone	Hot Chocolate
Drowning In Berlin	The Mobiles
What Have I Done To Deserve This?	Pet Shop Boys and Dusty Springfield
What Difference Does It Make?	The Smiths
My Toot Toot	Denise LaSalle
Happy Talk	Captain Sensible
Build	The Housemartins
Nirvana	The Cult
Passing Strangers	Ultravox
The Bed's Too Big Without You	The Police
Soldier's Things	Paul Young

Show 26

Mothers Talk	Tears For Fears
I Could Never Take The Place Of Your Man	Prince
Heart (Stop Beating In Time)	Leo Sayer
Jenifa Taught Me (Derwin's Revenge)	De La Soul
Duel	Propaganda
Love Is A Battlefield	Pat Benatar
Strange Little Girl	Sad Café
Don't Mess With Me	Karyn White
Waiting For Another Chance	Endgames
Hit The Ground	The Darling Buds
This Corrosion	Sisters of Mercy
Tomb of Memories	Paul Young
Why Can't I Be You?	The Cure
I Could Show You How	Naked Eyes
Sign O' The Times	The Belle Stars
Freak	Bruce Foxton
New Amsterdam	Elvis Costello
A Question of Time	Depeche Mode
The Right Stuff	Bryan Ferry

Rattlesnakes	Lloyd Cole and The Commotions
Best Friend	The Beat
Rapture	Blondie
Anchorage	Shocked
Tom's Diner	Suzanne Vega
Stay Gold	Stevie Wonder

Show 27

The Telephone Always Rings	Fun Boy Three
Icing on The Cake	Stephen 'Tin Tin' Duffy
Cross That Bridge	The Ward Brothers
St. Elmo's Fire (Man In Motion)	John Parr
Boys of Summer	Don Henley
Rosanna	Toto
Freebird	Will To Power
Never Never	The Assembly
Grimly Fiendish	The Damned
You Don't Love Me	Marilyn
The Way It Is	Bruce Hornsby & The Range
Jump	Van Halen
Kyrie	Mr. Mister
To Be A Lover	Billy Idol
You're History	Shakespear's Sister
Mandinka	Sinead O'Connor
Hard Habit To Break	Chicago
The Minute I Saw You	John Parr
The Wedding List	Kate Bush
Believe It or Not	Joey Scarbury
The Gambler	Kenny Rogers
The Crown	Gary Byrd

Show 28

To Cut A Long Story Short	Spandau Ballet
Belle of St. Mark	Sheila E
Weak In The Presence of Beauty	Alison Moyet
Valley Girl	Frank Zappa
Don't Change	INXS
Twilight Zone	Golden Earring
El Dorado	Drum Theatre
Blue Hat For A Blue Day	Nick Heyward
Prospect Street	The Big Dish
More, More, More	Carmel
Words	Missing Persons

Never Say Never	Romeo Void
Games Without Frontiers	Peter Gabriel
Like Flames	Berlin
How Men Are	Aztec Camera
At The Edge	Stiff Little Fingers
Don't Try To Stop It	Roman Holliday
The Walk	The Cure
Love Will Tear Us Apart	Joy Division
Why Me?	Planet P
Some People	Cliff Richard
Who's Gonna Catch You	Mel and Kim
Never Underestimate	
The Ignorance of The Rich	Klaxon 5
These Dreams	Heart
Hi-Fidelity	Kids From Fame

Show 29

Rabbit	Chas 'n' Dave
Fool's Paradise	Mel'isa Morgan
Julie Thru The Blinds	The Jeremy Days
The Honeythief	Hipsway
The Killing Moon	Echo & The Bunnymen
The Message	Grand Master Flash and The Furious Five
No Fool (For Love)	Hazell Dean
Friends Will Be Friends	Queen
Be There	Clive Griffin
Foolin' Yourself	Paul Hardcastle
Happiness Is Easy	Talk Talk
Party Fears 2	The Associates
Fool For Your Loving	Whitesnake
Ask Johnny Dee	The Chesterfields
Magic Smile	Rosie Vela
Ship of Fools	Erasure
Hurry Home	Wavelength
Train of Thought	A-ha
Tinseltown In The Rain	The Blue Nile
Kissing A Fool	George Michael
Human's Lib	Howard Jones
Miracle of Love	Eurythmics
Save It	Immaculate Fools

Show 30

Ruby Tuesday	Julian Lennon

Girlfriend	Pebbles
Do The Right Thing	Redhead Kingpin & The FBI
Never Gonna Give You Up	Musical Youth
Don't Worry, Be Happy	Bobby McFerrin
Livin' On A Prayer	Bon Jovi
Let My Love Open The Door	Pete Townshend
In Your Car	The Cool Notes
Angel	Madonna
Life In One Day	Howard Jones
When Doves Cry	Prince
Every Breath You Take	The Police
Big Apple	Kajagoogoo
Can't Get Used To Losing You	The Beat
Everything's Coming Up Roses	Black
Family Man	Roachford
Danger Games	The Pinkees
Glittering Prize	Simple Minds
Goodbye To You	Scandal
Buffalo Soldier	Bob Marley
Youth of Today	Musical Youth
More Than A Party	Depeche Mode
In Private	Dusty Springfield
Shiny Shiny	Haysi Fantayzee
Walking on The Chinese Wall	Philip Bailey

Show 31

Ferry 'Cross The Mersey	Gerry Marsden, Paul McCartney, Holly Johnson and The Christians
Free Yourself	The Untouchables
You Can't Hide (Your Love From Me)	David Joseph
Pleased To Meet You	Owen Paul
Where The Streets Have No Name	U2
Slave To The Rhythm	Grace Jones
101-Dam-Nations	Scarlet Party
I Don't Want Your Love	Duran Duran
Hand Held In Black And White	Dollar
Do You Believe In Love	Huey Lewis and The News
Themes For Great Cities	Simple Minds
A Different Corner	George Michael
I'm Falling	The Bluebells
Passionate Friend	The Teardrop Explodes
Good Thing Going	Sugar Minott
Marguerita Time	Status Quo
I Thank You	Adeva

Partyman	Prince
Duel	Propaganda
January February	Barbara Dickson
When The Angels	Prefab Sprout
Night Train	Visage
Lay All Your Love On Me	Abba
Something Inside So Strong	Labi Siffre

Show 32

Desdemona	Kids From Fame
Panic	The Smiths
Friday On My Mind	Gary Moore
Don't Leave Me This Way	The Communards
Come On Eileen	Dexys Midnight Runners
Slow Love	Prince
I Want To Be Straight	Ian Dury & The Blockheads
Eyes Without A Face	Billy Idol
King for A Day	Thompson Twins
Since You're Gone	the Cars
My Ever Changing Moods	The Style Council
The Piano Has Been Drinking	Tom Waits
Can't Stop The Music	The Village People
Eighties	Killing Joke
Iko Iko	The Belle Stars
What's The Colour of Money	Hollywood Beyond
Sleepwalk	Ultravox
Mirror Man	Human League
Don't Give Up	Peter Gabriel and Kate Bush
Bare My Soul	Sarah Jane Morris
Sweet Thing	Yazoo
Please, Please, Please	
Let Me Get What I Want	Dream Academy
Alice, I Want You Just For Me	Full Force
This Is England	The Clash

Show 33

Dance Yourself Dizzy	Liquid Gold
Rage To Love	Kim Wilde
Rock 'n' Roll Mercenaries	Meatloaf and John Parr
Planet Claire	B52's
Nobody's Fool	Haircut 100
I'll House You	Jungle Brothers
Back In Black	AC/DC
Undercover of The Night	The Rolling Stones

Who's Leaving Who	Hazell Dean
Take Good Care of My Heart	Jermaine Jackson ft. Whitney Houston
Drowning in Berlin	The Mobiles
Looking for Clues	Robert Palmer
The Irish Rover	The Pogues and The Dubliners
She Can't Wait	S.P.Y.S.
Sick of It	The Primitives
Saved By Zero	The Fixx
Love Machine	Wham!
Sunset Now	Heaven 17
Love Is In Control	Donna Summer
High Life	Modern Romance
Where's The Party?	Madonna
Temptation	Wet Wet Wet
Star	Kiki Dee
Bass (How Low Can You Go)	Simon Harris

Show 34

All Night Holiday	Russ Abbott
Dance	The Lambrettas
Half A Boy And Half A Man	Nick Lowe
East of The River	Wet Wet Wet
Drive	The Cars
Cloudbusting	Kate Bush
Flight of Icarus	Iron Maiden
Down On The Street	Shakatak
P Machinery	Propaganda
Diggi-Loo Diggi-Ley	Herrey's
Rapture	Blondie
Tempted	Squeeze
For Your Eyes Only	Sheena Easton
Tired of Getting Pushed Around	Two Men, A Drum Machine and a Trumpet
Kool In The Kaftan	B. A. Robertson
18 Carat Love Affair	The Associates
Jamaican Sunrise	We've Got A Fuzzbox And We're Gonna Use It
We Belong Together	Los Lobos
The Kingdom	Icehouse
Freefallin'	Tom Petty
Solitude Standing	Suzanne Vega
Never Take Me Alive	Spear of Destiny

Show 35

Warning Sign	Nick Heyward
This Is The Shirt	Two People
Puss 'n' Boots	Adam Ant
Liberator	Spear of Destiny
Police and Thieves	Junior Murvin
West One (Shine On Me)	The Ruts
Tenderness	General Public
Break My Stride	Matthew Wilder
Millionaire	Owen Paul
Overkill	Men At Work
Das Modell	Kraftwerk
You're Wondering Now	The Specials
All Tomorrow's Parties	Japan
Don't Box Me In	Stan Ridgway and Stewart Copeland
Rock & Roll Dreams Come Through	Jim Steinman
Backfired	Debbie Harry
I Can't Help It	Bananarama
Perfect Skin	Lloyd Cole and The Commotions
Tearproof	The Undertones
The Final Countdown	Europe
We Care A Lot	Faith No More
An Elegant Chaos	Julian Cope
Long Hot Summer	The Style Council
Walkin' In The Sunshine	Bad Manners
Wedding Bells	Godley and Creme

Show 36

Instinction	Spandau Ballet
Bitter Sweet	Marc Almond
When She Was My Girl	The Four Tops
Round And Around	Jaki Graham
Call Me	Go West
Sweet Freedom	Michael McDonald
Girl You're So Together	Michael Jackson
Hey Music Lover	S'Express
Major Tom (Coming Home)	Peter Schilling
Chinatown	Thin Lizzy
Easy Lover	Phillip Bailey and Phil Collins
I Knew You Were Waiting	Aretha Franklin and George Michael
Never Knew Love Like This	Alexander O'Neal ft. Cherelle

Ship of Fools	World Party
Slow Down	Loose Ends
Party In Paris	UK Subs
All In All	Joyce Sims
I'm In Love With A German Film Star	The Passions
Owner of A Lonely Heart	Yes
Just Making Memories	Black
Cold Dark and Yesterday	Hall & Oates
The Show (Theme From Connie)	Rebecca Storm
Theme From M*A*S*H (Suicide Is Painless)	M*A*S*H
Swan Lake	Madness

Show 37

Listen To Your Father	Feargal Sharkey
Going Back To My Roots	Odyssey
Coward of The County	Kenny Rogers
Shadow of Love	The Damned
Story of The Blues	Wah!
Nothing Looks The Same In The Light	Wham!
To Be A Lover	Billy Idol
Talking In Your Sleep	Bucks Fizz
Red Guitar	David Sylvian
Charlotte Sometimes	The Cure
Smalltown Boy	Bronski Beat
Shelter From The Rain	All About Eve
She Bop	Cyndi Lauper
Bad Day	Carmel
Paris Match	The Style Council
World Shut Your Mouth	Julian Cope
Nine While Nine	The Sisters of Mercy
Empty Rooms	Gary Moore
You Broke My Heart In 17 Places	Tracey Ullman
Rent	Pet Shop Boys
Gale Force Wind	Microdisney
Tossing and Turning	Windjammer
This Time	England Squad

Show 38

Welcome	Gino Latino
Boys and Girls	The Human League
This World of Water	New Musik
Can You Feel The Force	The Real Thing
Lovely Day	Bill Withers
Children of The Ghetto	Philip Bailey

Hanging Around With The Big Boys	Bloomsbury Set
Computer Game	Yellow Magic Orchestra
Mental Hopscotch	Missing Persons
There's No Stopping Us	Ollie & Jerry
After The Love Has Gone	Earth, Wind And Fire
Let's Do It Again	The Staple Sisters
Rain	The Cult
Indigo Eyes	Peter Murphy
Missing Words	The Selecter
Europa And The Pirate Twins	Thomas Dolby
Wishing Well	Terence Trent D'Arby
I've Been Losing You	A-ha
Love Won't Let Me Wait	Luther Vandross
Rain Or Shine	Five Star
A Matter of Feeling	Duran Duran
Summertime	Fun Boy Three

Show 39

Welcome To The Pleasuredome	Frankie Goes To Hollywood
Burst	The Darling Buds
Indian Summer	The Belle Stars
Stay Out Of My Life	Five Star
Alone	Heart
Dancing On The Ceiling	Lionel Ritchie
One Way Street	Go West
Heat of The Moment	Asia
Nobody Knows	Nik Kershaw
It's Over	The Funkmasters
I Found Lovin'	The Fatback Band
The Voice	John Farnham
Beyond The Pale	The Mission
Gimme 5	Jovanotti
Lover Come Back To Me	Dead or Alive
I Know There's Something Going On	Frida
Words	F. R. David
Surrender	Swing Out Sister
Black Velvet	Alannah Myles
Man Out Of Time	Elvis Costello
The Dive	Culture Club
I'll Sail This Ship Alone	Beautiful South
I Keep Forgetting	Michael McDonald
The Land of Make Believe	Bucks Fizz

Show 40

Club Tropicana	Wham!
Second Summer Of Love	Danny Wilson
Walkin' On Sunshine	Rockers Revenge
Just Who Is The 5 O'Clock Hero	The Jam
Life's What You Make It	Talk Talk
Headstart For Happiness	The Style Council
Fantasy Island	Tight Fit
Boys (Summertime Love)	Sabrina
Heat It Up	Wee Papa Girl Rappers
Tantalise	Jimmy The Hoover
Somewhere In My Heart	Aztec Camera
Let's Dance	David Bowie
Farewell My Summer Love	Michael Jackson
Fantastic Day	Haircut 100
The Caribbean Disco Show	Lobo
Twisting By The Pool	Dire Straits
Summer of '82	Fun Boy Three
Summer Fun	The Barracudas
Waiting On A Friend	The Rolling Stones
Drifting Dreams	From The Jam
A Ray of Sunshine	Wham!
Boys of Summer	Don Henley
Sunglasses	Tracey Ullman
Endless Summer Nights	Richard Marx

Show 41

Gloria	Laura Brannigan
Do You Dream In Colour	Bill Nelson
Body Language	Detroit Spinners
Under The Boardwalk	Tom Tom Club
Desdemona	Kids From Fame
Safety Dance	Men Without Hats
Rock & Roll Is King	ELO
Don't Dream It's Over	Crowded House
Calling All The Heroes	It Bites
Jump To It!	Heartbeat UK
Clouds Across The Moon	The Rah Band
Lean On Me	Red Box
The Boy Who Cried Wolf	The Style Council
Girlie Girlie	Sophia George
So In Love With You	Spear of Destiny
Give Me Back My Heart	Dollar
TV	The Flying Lizards

I Could Be So Good For You	Dennis Waterman
Love On The Run	The Human League
Come Home	James
Transformer Man	Neil Young
The Magician	Secession
Rat Race	The Specials
Never Say Goodbye	Bon Jovi

Show 42

Animation	The Skids
The Right Stuff	Vanessa Williams
See That Glow	This Island Earth
The Word Girl	Scritti Politti
Messages	OMD
Hey Little Girl	Icehouse
Can I Play With Madness	Iron Maiden
Over My Head	Toni Basil
Song For Whoever	Beautiful South
West One (Shine On Me)	The Ruts
I Don't Believe in You	Talk Talk
Ziggy Stardust	Bauhaus
Love Town	Booker Newbury III
See You	Depeche Mode
Whatcha Gonna Do For Me?	Jody Whatley
It's Over	Level 42
The Boy In The Bubble	Paul Simon
Ninety In The Shade	Little Angels
Madam Butterfly	Malcolm McLaren
Cool Under Heat	The Clash
Code of Love	Spandau Ballet
To Know Someone Deeply Is To Know Someone Softly	Terence Trent D'Arby
Down The Dip	Aztec Camera
Freeway of Love	Aretha Franklin

Show 43

The first anniversary show featured a playlist predominantly chosen by former Favourite Five guests. Their name appears in italics under their song choice.

Celebration	Kool & The Gang
Rhythm of The Jungle	The Quick *(Andy Kyriacou)*
And The Beat Goes On	The Whispers *(Junior Giscombe)*

Breakout	Swing Out Sister
	(Dennis Seaton)
Don't Stop 'Til You Get Enough	Michael Jackson
	(Dave Barbarossa)
I Ran	A Flock of Seagulls
	(Steve Blacknell)
Super Freak	Rick James
	(Grahame Skinner)
First We Take Manhattan	Leonard Cohen
Imagination	Belouis Some
	(Nick van Eede)
Somebody Else's Guy	Jocelyn Brown
	(Bobby McVay)
Special Brew	Bad Manners
	(Max Splodge)
(You Gotta) Fight For Your Right (To Party)	Beastie Boys
	(Clive Jackson)
Never Too Much	Luther Vandross
	(Chris Amoo)
Just Can't Get Enough	Depeche Mode
	(Helen McCookerybook)
Happy Birthday	Stevie Wonder
	(Denise Pearson)
Ain't No Pleasing You	Chas 'n' Dave
Party Fears 2	The Associates
Fresh	Kool & The Gang
	(Karel Fialka)
Big Area	Then Jerico
	(Tracie Young)
Our House	Madness
	(Andy Overall)
It's My Party	Dave Stewart and
	Barbra Gaskin
Party In Paris	UK Subs
She's Strange	Cameo
	(David Brewis)
Anotherloverholeinyohead	Prince
	(Peter Coyle)
The Final Countdown	Europe
	(Kirk Brandon)

The Early Days

Before the My 80s show found its home on Mad Wasp Radio, it spent three months on Herne Bay's Radio Cabin. Listeners to those early shows will remember the technical problems we often had, such as the wrong tracks being loaded or the first hour of the show being repeated instead of the second hour airing. Despite the stress of wondering what was going to happen next, I am glad for my time there as not only did it get me started on the airwaves, but I learned how to record, edit and produce my shows. Even if it was out of necessity, it is something I'm glad I can now do, and it meant I was able to put together and introduce features like Monster Mash Up. Not bad for a self-confessed technophobe!

The following pages list the tracks I played during my days at Radio Cabin and, just like all the My 80s shows on Mad Wasp Radio, these shows can be found on Mixcloud. Search for Sarah Lewis #My80s.

Track   Artist

Show 1

Track	Artist
Election Day	Arcadia
Some Like It Hot	The Power Station
Dancing With Myself	Billy Idol
We Belong	Pat Benatar
Come Dancing	The Kinks
Confusion Hits Us Everytime	The Truth
Start	The Jam
Love's Great Adventure	Ultravox
Street Tuff	Double Trouble and The Rebel MC
Sonic Boom Boy	West World
I Want To Be Straight	Ian Dury and The Blockheads
You Will Always Find Me In The Kitchen At Parties	Jona Lewie
There's A Guy Works Down The Chip Shop Swears He's Elvis	Kirsty MacColl
Waterfront	Simple Minds
Left To My Own Devices	Pet Shop Boys
Born To Run	Frankie Goes To Hollywood
First Picture of You	The Lotus Eaters
I Dream To Sleep	H2O
Closest Thing To Heaven	The Kane Gang
When Will You Make My 'Phone Ring?	Deacon Blue
Fantasy Island	Tight Fit

Bedsitter	Soft Cell
White Lines	Grandmaster Flash and The Furious Five
Ordinary Girl	Alison Moyet
Everything Must Change	Paul Young
Too Nice To Talk To	The Beat
Since Yesterday	Strawberry Switchblade
Zoom	Fat Larry's Band

Show 2

Love Is A Wonderful Colour	Icicle Works
My World	Secret Affair
Margate	Chas 'n' Dave
Special Brew	Bad Manners
The Reflex	Duran Duran
Easy Lover	Phil Collins and Philip Bailey
Edge of Heaven	Wham!
Love Action	The Human League
Killer In The Home	Adam And The Ants
Imagination	Belouis Some
Walk This Way	Aerosmith with Run DMC
Sexual Healing	Marvin Gaye
Let's Dance	David Bowie
Hi-Fidelity	Kids From Fame
Drowning In Berlin	The Mobiles
It's A Hard Life	Queen
Immaculate Fools	Immaculate Fools
Back In Black	AC/DC
This Corrosion	Sisters of Mercy
Obsession	Animotion
Forbidden Colours	Ryuichi Sakamoto and David Sylvian
Pretty In Pink	Psychedelic Furs
Let's Go Round Again	Average White Band
Solsbury Hill	Peter Gabriel

Show 3

Good Life	Inner City
I Can't Wait	Nu Shooz
Jukebox (Don't Put Another Dime)	The Flirts
Dracula's Tango	Toto Coelo
Asylums In Jerusalem	Scritti Politti
Ay Ay Ay Ay Moosey	Modern Romance
Tunnel Of Love	Fun Boy Three

Thinking Of You	The Colourfield
This City Never Sleeps	Eurythmics
Take Me With U	Prince
It Must Be Love	Madness
Room In Your Heart	Living In A Box
Out In The Fields	Gary Moore and Phil Lynott
Shake The Disease	Depeche Mode
Cambodia	Kim Wilde
Friend or Foe	Adam And The Ants
Speak Like A Child	The Style Council
Alice, I Want You Just For Me	Full Force
Hands To Heaven	Breathe
Diamond Lights	Hoddle and Waddle
If She Knew What She Wants	The Bangles
My Camera Never Lies	Bucks Fizz
I'd Rather Jack	The Reynolds Girls
The Trumpton Riots	Half Man Half Biscuit
Memorabilia	Soft Cell
I Second That Emotion	Japan
Silver	Echo And The Bunnymen
Black Man Ray	China Crisis

Show 4

Calling Your Name	Marilyn
Do You Feel My Love	Eddy Grant
Spirit	Bauhaus
How Soon Is Now	The Smiths
Message of Love	The Pretenders
All Around The World	Lisa Stansfield
Buffalo Stance	Neneh Cherry
Drag Me Down	Boomtown Rats
Pass The Dutchie	Musical Youth
Don't Turn Around	Aswad
Roses Are Red	Mac Band
The Crown	Gary Byrd And The GB Experience
She's Leaving	OMD
Waiting For A Train	Flash And The Pan
Cover Me	Bruce Springsteen
John Wayne Is Big Leggy	Haysi Fantayzee
Stand Or Fall	The Fixx
Wait	Robert Howard and Kim Mazelle
Come On Eileen	Dexys Midnight Runners

Mirror In The Bathroom	The Beat
Many Rivers To Cross	UB40
What Kind Of Boy You Looking For (Girl)	Hot Chocolate
Ruder Than You	The Bodysnatchers
Just Like Heaven	The Cure
Why?	Carly Simon
Modern Girl	Meat Loaf
You Make My Dreams Come True	Hall & Oates

Show 5

Walkin' On Sunshine	Rockers Revenge
Cry Boy Cry	Blue Zoo
Eighth Day	Hazel O'Connor
What?	Soft Cell
Love Action	Human League
Burning Car	John Foxx
Visions In Blue	Ultravox
She Blinded Me With Science	Thomas Dolby
Up Around The Bend	Hanoi Rocks
Fade To Grey	Visage
(We Don't Need This) Fascist Groove Thang	Heaven 17
Atmosphere	Joy Division
Listen Like Thieves	INXS
Big Time	Peter Gabriel
Why Me?	Mike & The Mechanics
Duel	Propaganda
The Bucket of Water Song	The Four Bucketeers
What Have I Done To Deserve This	Pet Shop Boys and Dusty Springfield
Hand In Glove	Sandie Shaw and The Smiths
Let The Music Play	Shannon
This Ole House	Shakin' Stevens
This House	Big Sound Authority
Broken Land	The Adventures
Jessie's Girl	Rick Springfield
Madam Butterfly	Malcolm McLaren

Show 6

Rockin' All Over The World	Status Quo
Just Got Lucky	Jo Boxers
Where were You Hiding When The Storm Broke?	The Alarm
Two Tribes	Frankie Goes To Hollywood
The Downtown Lights	The Blue Nile

Life's What You Make It	Talk Talk
No More I Love Yous	The Lover Speaks
Appetite	Prefab Sprout
Love Makes The World Go Round	Madonna
Here I Stand And Face The Rain	A-ha
Shipbuilding	Elvis Costello
Rush Hour	Jane Wiedlin
9 to 5	Dolly Parton
Night Train	Visage
I Can Dream About You	Dan Hartman
Wordy Rappinghood	Tom Tom Club
Just Sounds Like Noise	Brian Nash
Blue Monday	New Order
The Umpire Strikes Back	The Brat
Zulu Beat	King Kurt
(Forever) Live And Die	OMD
Violently	Hue and Cry
Sister of Mercy	Thompson Twins

Show 7

It's A Miracle	Culture Club
Blind Vision	Blancmange
Slide	The Big Dish
Do You Believe In Love	Huey Lewis and The News
Just Outside of Heaven	H2O
Slave To Love	Bryan Ferry
Quiet Life	Japan
Shakti (The Meaning Within)	Monsoon
(You Are My) All And All	Joyce Sims
The Chauffeur	Duran Duran
Drive	The Cars
Absolute Beginners	David Bowie
Absolute Beginners	The Jam
Heartline	Robin George
The Number of The Beast	Iron Maiden
Heaven	Psychedelic Furs
Let Love In	Ian Donaldson
Loverboy	Billy Ocean
Ai No Corrida	Quincy Jones
To Be A Lover	Billy Idol
Tragedy And Mystery	China Crisis
I Want To Hear It From You	Go West
When Am I Going To Make A Living	Sade
Wednesday Week	The Undertones

Show 8

Be With You	The Bangles
Do Ya Wanna Funk	Sylvester
Situation	Yazoo
Flashback	Imagination
Endless Love	Diana Ross and Lionel Richie
Girl You Need A Change of Mind	Eddie Kendricks
Mr. Solitaire	Animal Nightlife
Magic	The Cars
Jenifa Taught Me (Derwin's Revenge)	De La Soul
That's When I Think of You	1927
Say Say Say	Paul McCartney and Michael Jackson
Show Me	ABC
Me and Baby Brother	War
Inseparable	Natalie Cole
I'm No Rebel	View From The Hill
Breakfast	The Associates
Radio Head	Talking Heads
Seven Seas	Echo & The Bunnymen
What's Going On	Marvin Gaye
Do It Right Now	Leee John
But Not Tonight	Depeche Mode
Music For Chameleons	Gary Numan
I'll Be Good	Rene and Angela
One Step Further	Bardo
All Of My Life	Phil Collins

Show 9

The Wheel	Spear Of Destiny
This Wheel's On Fire	Siouxsie and The Banshees
Being Boiled	The Human League
Shattered Dreams	Johnny Hates Jazz
Forbidden Colours	David Sylvian and Ryuichi Sakamoto
Life's What You Make It	Talk Talk
For Spacious Lies	Norman Cook ft. Lester
Shout To The Top	Style Council
Stereotype	The Specials
Is Vic There?	Department S
Sowing The Seeds Of Love	Tears For Fears
Don't Dream It's Over	Crowded House
Someone Somewhere In Summertime	Simple Minds
Sanctum Sanctorum	The Damned

You Gave Me Love — Crown Heights Affair
Comment Te Dire Adieu — Jimmy Somerville with
June Miles-Kingston

Silent Running — Mike and The Mechanics
Arc Of A Diver — Steve Winwood
Nine Hours — Peter and Toyah
Sweetest Smile — Black
Never Tear Us Apart — INXS
Land Of Make Believe — Bucks Fizz

Show 10

Woman Of The 80s — Julia Fordham
Lorraine — Bad Manners
Love Is The Slug — We've Got A Fuzzbox And
We're Gonna Use It

Mama Used To Say — Junior
I'm In Love — Evelyn King
Never Too Much — Luther Vandross
The More You Live The More You Love — A Flock Of Seagulls
The Telephone Always Rings — Fun Boy Three
Dumb Things — Paul Kelly
No Rest — New Model Army
Skin Trade — Duran Duran
Let Your Feeling Show — Earth, Wind & Fire
Don't Let It Go To Your Head — Jean Carn
Thunder In The Mountains — Toyah
Life Is A Celebration — Kids From Fame
Open Your Eyes — Lords of The New Church
Maggie — B.A. Robertson
Pour Some Sugar on Me — Def Leppard
Drop The Pilot — Joan Armatrading
Ribbon In The Sky — Stevie Wonder
Another Step — Kim Wilde and Junior
Circus Ring — Vitamin Z
Wide Boy — Nik Kershaw
My Secret Garden — Depeche Mode
Spirits (Having Flown) — Bee Gees

Show 11

Head Over Heels — The Go-Go's
Free Fallin' — Tom Petty
I Beg Your Pardon — Kon Kan
I Just Died In Your Arms Tonight — Cutting Crew
Pale Shelter — Tears for Fears

Whole of the Moon	The Waterboys
East Of Eden	Big Country
Flag Day	Housemartins
I'm Not The Man I Used To Be	Fine Young Cannibals
One Better Day	Madness
Carnation	The Jam
Need You Tonight	INXS
Self Control	Laura Brannigan
Change of Heart	Cyndi Lauper
Save It For Later	The Beat
Blue Hotel	Chris Isaak
I Still Haven't Found What I'm Looking For	U2
Berlin In Winter	Cutting Crew
When We Were Young	Bucks Fizz
Careful	Horse
When Your Heart Was Young	The Adventures
Nothing Can Divide Us	Jason Donovan
Inside Out	The Mighty Lemon Drops
Never Never	The Assembly

Show 12

Ask	The Smiths
Don't Look Down	Go West
Right Now	The Creatures
Every Day I Write The Book	Elvis Costello
Into The Groove	Madonna
Mountains	Prince
There It Is	Shalamar
Take That Look Off Your Face	Marti Webb
Round And Round	Spandau Ballet
Black Coffee In Bed	Squeeze
Wishing (If I Had A Photograph of You)	A Flock Of Seagulls
Bridges	Tracey Chapman
Jessie's Girl	Rick Springfield
Eloise	The Damned
Let Me Down Easy	The Stranglers
Caravan Of Love	Isley Jasper Isley
Comin' On Strong	Broken English
Dear Jessie	Madonna
Dirty Back Road	B52s
Razzmatazz	Quincy Jones
April Skies	Jesus And Mary Chain
You'll Never Be So Wrong	Hot Chocolate
All At Once	Whitney Houston

Don't Try To Stop It	Roman Holliday
Last Night Another Soldier	Angelic Upstarts

Show 13

Farewell My Summer Love	Michael Jackson
Fantasy Island	Tight Fit
Island of Lost Souls	Blondie
IOU	Freeez
Electric Youth	Debbie Gibson
The Crown	Gary Byrd
The Knowledge	Janet Jackson
Warning Sign	Nick Heyward
Clouds Across The Moon	The Rah Band
E=MC2	Big Audio Dynamite
You Think You're A Man	Divine
Ain't No Pleasing You	Chas 'n' Dave
New Life	Depeche Mode
Hey DJ (I Can't Dance To That)	Beatmasters ft Betty Boo
Dancing With Myself	Generation X
Tarzan Boy	Baltimora
Pleased To Meet You	Owen Paul
Just A Mirage	Jellybean
Happy Talk	Captain Sensible
Live It Up	Mental As Anything
Enola Gay	OMD
Tears Of A Clown	The Beat
And The Beat Goes On	The Whispers
Thank You For The Music	Abba

Back On Track

Show 1 08/06/2017
"Born To Run" by Frankie Goes To Hollywood from "Welcome To The Pleasuredome"

Show 2 15/06/2017
"Killer In The Home" by Adam And The Ants from "Kings of The Wild Frontier"

Show 3 22/06/2017
"This City Never Sleeps" by Eurythmics from "Sweet Dreams"

Show 4 29/06/2017
"She's Leaving" by OMD from "Architecture & Morality"

Show 5 06/07/2017
"Why Me?" by Mike & The Mechanics from "The Living Years"

Show 6 13/07/2017
"Here I Stand And Face The Rain" by A-ha from "Hunting High And Low"

Show 7 20/07/2017
"The Chauffeur" by Duran Duran from "Rio"

Show 8 27/07/2017
"Show Me" by ABC from "The Lexicon of Love"

Show 9 03/08/2017
"Sanctum Sanctorum" by The Damned from "Phantasmagoria"

Show 10 10/08/2017
"My Secret Garden" by Depeche Mode from "A Broken Frame"

Show 11 17/08/2017
"When Your Heart Was Young" by The Adventures from "The Sea of Love"

Show 12 24/08/2017
"Dirty Back Road" by B52s from "Wild Planet"

Show 13 31/08/2017
"The Knowledge" by Janet Jackson from "Rhythm Nation 1814"

Word Up

Show 9 03/08/2017
"Sweetest SMILE" by Black

Show 10 10/08/2017
"THUNDER In The Mountains" by Toyah

Show 11 17/08/2017
"Blue HOTEL" by Chris Isaak

Show 12 24/08/2017
"Black COFFEE In Bed" by Squeeze

Show 13 31/08/2017
"DANCING With Myself" by Generation X

Make It Big

The first few shows on Radio Cabin included this feature in which listeners chose a 12" single. These were the choices:

Show 1 "White Lines" by Grandmaster Flash and The Furious Five
Show 2 "Obsession" by Animotion
Show 3 "Memorabilia" by Soft Cell
Show 4 "Why?" by Carly Simon
Show 5 "Let The Music Play" by Shannon
Show 6 "Wordy Rappinghood" by Tom Tom Club
Show 7 "To Be A Lover" by Billy Idol
Show 8 "Radio Head" by Talking Heads

Favourite Five

Show 2 15/06/2017
Andy Kyriacou
The former Modern Romance drummer may now front the band but he hasn't lost his rhythm, as we found out when he spoke about his final song choice.

"The Reflex" by Duran Duran
"Easy Lover" by Phil Collins & Phillip Bailey
"Sexual Healing" by Marvin Gaye
"Let's Dance" by David Bowie
"Walk This Way" by Aerosmith

Show 4 29/06/2017
Dennis Seaton
Musical Youth's lead singer is proud of his Birmingham roots and selected a number of fellow Brummies in his Favourite Five.

"Don't Turn Around" by Aswad
"Roses Are Red" by The Mac Band
"Come On Eileen" by Dexys Midnight Runners
"Mirror In The Bathroom" by The Beat
"Many Rivers To Cross" by UB40

Show 5 06/07/2017
David Ball
Soft Cell's keyboard player and song writer sounded like he was in an underwater dungeon during our interview, due to technical issues during recording.

"Love Action" by The Human League
"Burning Car" by John Foxx

"Fade To Grey" by Visage
"(We Don't Need This) Fascist Groove Thang" by Heaven 17
"Duel" by Propaganda

Show 6 13/07/2017
Brian Nash
Frankie Goes To Hollywood's former guitarist spoke about prostitutes, cocaine and recording his audio book when he appeared on the show.

"The Downtown Lights" by The Blue Nile
"Life's What You Make It" by Talk Talk
"Shipbuilding" by Elvis Costello
"Rush Hour" by Jane Wiedlin
"Blue Monday" by New Order

Show 7 20/07/2017
Ian Donaldson
We were treated to the unmistakable tones of the former H2O lead singer, playing the Scots' latest solo release after his final Favourite Five choice.

"Slave To Love" by Bryan Ferry
"Quiet Life" by Japan
"Drive" by The Cars
"Absolute Beginners" by David Bowie
"Heaven" by Psychedelic Furs

Show 8 27/07/2017
Leee John
The Imagination singer took a step back from the Eighties, choosing his all-time Favourite Five songs when he joined us on the feature.

"Endless Love" by Diana Ross and Lionel Richie
"Girl You Need A Change of Mind" by Eddie Kendricks
"Me and Baby Brother" by War
"Inseparable" by Natalie Cole
"What's Going On" by Marvin Gaye

Show 9 03/08/2017
Clark Datchler
Thirty years on from the release of the 'Turn Back The Clock', the Johnny Hates Jazz lead singer and songwriter spoke about performing the album live again, when he made his song selection.

"Forbidden Colours" by David Sylvian and Ryuichi Sakamoto

"Life's What You Make It" by Talk Talk
"Sowing The Seeds Of Love" by Tears For Fears
"Don't Dream It's Over" by Crowded House
"Silent Running" by Mike & The Mechanics

Show 10 10/08/2017
Junior Giscombe
I bent the rules a little when the 'Mama Used To Say' singer made his choices. Not only was he too lovely to refuse but Junior told a beautiful story about his late daughter, Jenique, and dedicated his last Favourite Five choice to her.

"I'm In Love" by Evelyn King
"Never Too Much" by Luther Vandross
"Let Your Feeling Show" by Earth, Wind & Fire
"Don't Let It Go To Your Head" by Jean Carn
"Ribbon In The Sky" by Stevie Wonder

Show 11 17/08/2017
Nick Van Eede
Cutting Crew's lead singer revealed the ups and downs of song writing, and his struggle to settle on his of five tracks, when he spoke about his selection.

"Pale Shelter" by Tears for Fears
"The Whole of the Moon" by The Waterboys
"Carnation" by The Jam
"Need You Tonight" by INXS
"I Still Haven't Found What I'm Looking For" by U2

Show 12 24/08/2017
Jamie Days
Anyone who has read his 80's diaries is aware of this writer's love for Madonna, so it was no surprise when the Queen of Pop flanked the choice of tracks from Yorkshire's answer to Adrian Mole.

"Into The Groove" by Madonna"
"Mountains" by Prince
"Wishing (I Had A Photograph Of You)" by A Flock Of Seagulls
"Bridges" by Tracey Chapman
"Dear Jessie" by Madonna

My 80s Crossword

All the clues relate to songs and artists featured on the show

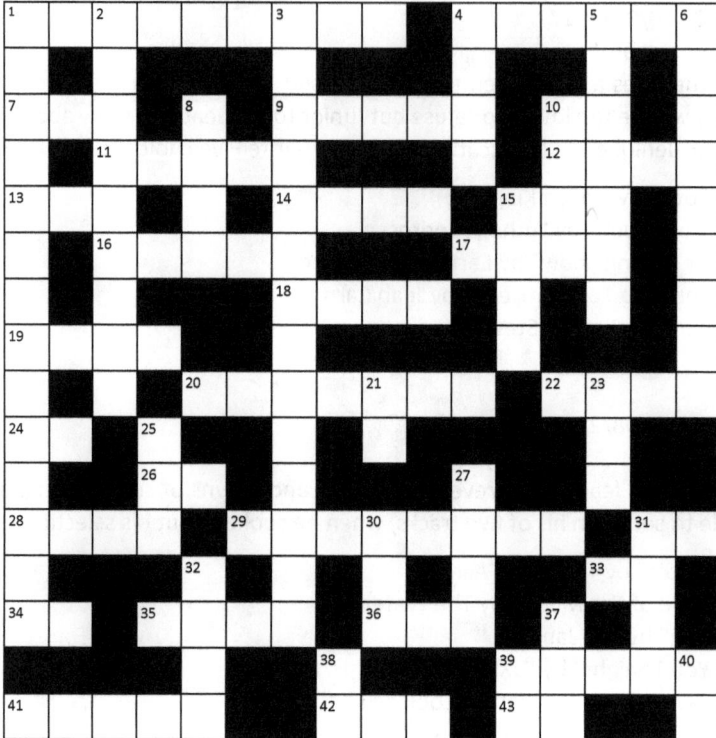

Across

1 Cockney duo who like to rabbit

4 See 1 down

7 & 4 down, 34 across, 43 across, 23 down Irene Cara song from the Fame soundtrack (3,4,2,2,3)

9 & 15 across, 27 down Luther Vandross couldn't get enough (5,3,4)

10 Initially, she sang with the Banshees (1,1)

11 See 28 across

12 Kate Bush had a wedding one (4)

13 Heaven Only Knows the initials of this illuminating band (1,1,1)

14 Mr Diamond's love was on the rocks (4)

15 See 9 across

16 The Ramones remembered a rock 'n' roll one (5)

17 See 10 down

18 John was a man in motion (4)

19 They sang about Rosanna (4)

20 & 35 across Geordie trio comprising of David Brewis, Paul Woods and Martin Brammer (3,4,4)

22 Innocent Billy sang about Christie Lee (4)

24 & 25 down, 37 down Howard Jones's advice on how not to live life (2,3,3)

26 Initially, he colour-coordinated his hat with the day (1,1)

28 & 31 across, 32 down, 38 down, 11 across Return an organ to Dollar? (4,2,4,2,5)

29 & 2 down They sang about This House in 1985 (3,5,9)

31 See 28 across

33 Mr Robertson sang about Maggie (1,1)

34 See 7 across

35 See 20 across

36 With or without an exclamation mark and sometimes mighty (3)

39 See 8 down

41 See 8 down

42 See 3 down

43 See 7 across

Down

1 & 4 across Biggest single chart success for 20 across (7,5,2,6)

2 See 29 across

3 & 42 across 1982 No. 2 hit for 1 across (4,2,8,3)

4 See 7 across

5 Ultravox had them in blue (7)

6 Vanity 6 sang about this unpleasant female (5,4)

8 & 39 across, 40 down, 41 across Chicago song is difficult to give up (4,5,2,5)

10 & 17 across Loose Ends take it easy (4,4)

15 James or Hadley (4)

21 Initially, they told us how men are (1,1)

23 See 7 across

25 See 24 across

27 See 9 across

30 Hit Factory producing trio in brief (1,1,1)

31 First name of Miss Beehive who cried a river (4)

32 See 28 across

37 See 24 across

38 See 28 across

39 Initially, she was a founder member of The Chefs (1,1)

40 See 8 down

Answers at back of book

Show Notes

My 80s was originally broadcast on Thursday evenings 9 to 11pm. However, the show moved to its current Sunday night slot 7 to 9pm on 17th December, 2017 (Show 15), following requests by many listeners to fill a void that had been left when another station's 80's show moved to a later time.

My 80s had been broadcast weekly for almost a year when other commitments and demands on my time meant I had to make a decision about its future. Every show takes far many more hours in researching, interviewing, recording, editing, etc. than the two hours it is broadcast for, and it was time I no longer had. I didn't want to give up the show as it is something I love doing, and I know many people look forward to listening to it. So, I had a chat with my fellow Mad Wasp presenter, Alan Read, and asked how he felt about sharing the Sunday night slot with me. My lovely quiz master agreed it was a good idea so, on 13th May 2018, Alan's Sequins To Suburbs show, an excellent mix of the finest 70's sounds, sidled in alongside My 80s. Our shows are now aired on alternate weeks at 7pm on Sunday on Mad Wasp Radio, and repeated on the station the following Tuesday (11am), Thursday (3am) and Saturday (2pm).

Answers

```
N R J K W A H S K A J G R A H M K I N
I E U G R E N N I K S E M A H A R G S
K N N S Y D S X N P K I R B Y G N S E
K N I T S E L U A P A H U J M Y O D E
E G O Y J E T J O A R A S A I R D N D
R X R S U N L L N U R T S K R I K V E
S N G T N A O L U L J N L G E A I K V
S Y I O I V H G H A O G F R B D C N A
W S S C M K N F X A H S O D R Y N R N
R T C E K C M Y K N S X X N A R R A U
A O O D E I A D I N Y T O O N A U L O
P W M D I N H D E B P D I S P G I S C
A A B L A N A E Y L N S R N U J O C A
U H E R N E R O X A S C H D G E M J I
L U C U N R G I R N B O M N D S B U R
A O U S B S I B I D J M B R A K O N Y
B C O L L S K R H A M B P K O B C I K
Y L A D Y R A G G R A E A P R R S O Y
A G R A I H J N K H M W R S N I R G D
L A Y K O A N D Y W A H S R E K K I N
D N R I A C U O K H A S T I G N O D A
```

Favourite Five

No. 1

```
K A R L D E A K L A I F L E R A K A N
I F E E E N I S L D A V I D B M A L L
A L R E L H C T A D K R A L C U C M L
A K F E P E A R B L Y O C W O S A C A
P T O J S S O N D P E T L I Y T Y V B
E T N O S L I W I R A M A L L A D A D
T E P H B D A S V K R H R S E F I V A
E R S N O Y N O A A E E K O N A J E N
N K L E E E R N D L E L E N O C O N N
A A I L K L J E E J E E R N S M L O N
G F W I L S O N K H B L D C D A G S Y
L D A J N N H E Y O N Y C R L R A R N
O E M T E R N B B M O O A E A A N A N
C N Y Y S K A B E U N C T L N I R E E
Y I B A C U Y D R S S R C H O R K P J
N I B Y V M M Y O T D E F M D A D E C
N S O B C A W N K N L T I B N M A S O
E E B V R R I I A A A E K A A E T I L
J P A E R S O N N K I P A L I E L N G
O Y C L R K S O F F R E R L K L E E A
N S D L A N O D N A I E J O H N R D H
```

Favourite Five

No. 2

Back On Track Anagrams: 1. An Elegant Chaos by Julian Cope 2. Tread Water by De La Soul 3. This City Never Sleeps by Eurythmics 4. Killer In The Home by Adam And The Ants 5. Hold Me Now by The Adventures 6. When The Angels by Prefab Sprout 7. Human's Lib by Howard Jones 8. Find A Reason by River City People 9. Wallflower by Peter Gabriel 10. Reeling by Then Jerico 11. The Knowledge by Janet Jackson 12. My Secret Garden by Depeche Mode 13. Christie Lee by Billy Joel 14. Sanctum Sanctorum by The Damned 15. The Wedding List by Kate Bush

Back On Track

```
A G O T Y T R A P E H T S E R E H W T
M I S W R R G R E A T P R O M I S A A
A T I H T A H E A R T B A T E B M S L
N D T E O S P A R T Y E M G D A K H K
O A T R W W W A H E L O V E N E L O T
F M O E T Y M E R R O T H O M M A W M
G E G S R T A E T T V E F R L O T M O
R T I T H E P S N I Y G I V G T N A E
P R O M I S S E W V R A N A T T I D K
O L O G E W D G I E R A E H T H R S K
M E V N M E O O A D E T W R T I V E I
T N I I O E M T K A T T P A Y N A W N
A G I H T T P M I M O R T E E G N H G
E K L A T R O O N T M E R H W N A E M
B I N G O M D D G I E A H T I A W R O
T N A M N I I N I T A L K A R N S E D
R A I W I A A V R O I N I E I N G K O
A S H O K N M O D G N I K B N V N I M
E I M E G A L O V E I T S I R A I N I
H I T E M O T K L A T H I N G N D O M
G R E A T M A N I S E P R O M A N A R
```

My 80s

```
M F U O R D P Q U E S T F I V E S R O
O A O D E T E U W A S P R E Q U P D W
N V P U H S A M R E T S N O M S E Q U
S U O O M I P A D U O L S C I A C C R
T P H L O X L C U D G U E T X R A T E
C R K C A R T N O K C A B M H A L S S
K A A X W A S M A D W A A O X E G U E
B T R I F R T Q U I Z P S N T V B E Q
A C K M I A E R E S M S S R I A R S
C H A R A S V T S A S A I T A F C R V
K N A M S L W O S T R F S R C E K T I
K O S H S P E C I A L G U E S T O N F
C T M W P A C K H U M V K M T I L A T
A R O A U O R L X I R Z C A S R E C I
W X N L D W E A O L C I I S E U W K X
A I S C W W O R D U P T T U U O W I R
S M E C I L A H L E W F S P Q V O S U
P P T S P E C S R I S I M H E A R A O
S G T H W V L U P U P V Z I R F D R V
E S R A M I O N S T R E U X S A W H A
U Q E R A T S M Z I U Q X C L O U D F
```

Word Up Anagrams: 1. So Cold The Night by The Communards 2. Dancing With Myself by Billy Idol 3. The Second Summer of Love by Danny Wilson 4. Don't Be Afraid of The Dark by Robert Cray Band 5. Down on The Street by Shakatak 6. Undercover of The Night by The Rolling Stones 7.Never Never by The Assembly 8. White Boy by Culture Club 9. Hazy Shade of Winter by The Bangles 10. A Winter's Tale by David Essex 11. Rapture by Blondie 12. Big In Japan by Alphaville 13. Hey Music Lover by S'Express 14. Dreamtime by Hall and Oates 15. A Good Year For The Roses by Elvis Costello

Word Up

```
A Y O N B R E A K M Y T R I S E D F I
L B O M R K O O L E H T T O G U A E R
L N M N B I T T T R A E H F I R Y E W
O E A A O H S E G A A L L M F E M M O
F W T M Y W T R A C R U O Y N I N A M
M M R O Y I R P M O C G O E E W O G B
Y O A W S R D U E I L S K I S S I R N
H O E E W G A T T L E W G O E H E E A
W N W R E A P N C M S E O N E A R T M
H O E I E M C O O S W E T A K H T U O
I N N F T E M S M I E T U M S E S P W
T M E N E P A N P R S E Y R W A M M F
B O Y A S M I L U T R S T Y E R I O R
U N A F T I R Y T E T T I A N T L C E
G D M I S S I O N R Y S A M E A E A I
O A O R M S N A I W O M N A T L O R H
T Y W E L I O D R F U I Y P U L E H T
T M O O N O E Y C A R L C O M F K O T
H C O M P T E R Y O B E T I H W G O O
E R E T U S N E W M O N D A Y M O L G
K S W E T E T R A E H Y M F O L L A U
```

Favourite Five Crossword

Across: 1. The Colour Of 7. Ball 9. Happiness 10. Spring 11. Spurs 12. 15 13. TT (Talk Talk) 14. Wilko 15. My 16. Tracie 20. PC (Peter Coyle) 21. NK (Nik Kershaw) 22. RSPB 24. Mari 27. Young 30. Or 31. Should 32. Out 33. Arrow 35. LJ (Leee John) 36. LA (Love Action) 37. Hello 39. Bangs 41. Guns 42. Yes

Down: 2. Headstart For 3. Cyprus 4. Owen 5. Russell 6. Fashion 7. Burning Car 8. Land 14. WO (West One) 15. Mind 17. CA (Chris Amoo) 18. ER (Eddie Roxy) 19. EP 23. Brooklyn 24. Mull 25. I Go 26. Aztec 27. Youth 28. Girl On 29. A Swing 33. All 34. Jane 36. Lay 38. EM (Erkan Mustafa) 40. GS (Grahame Skinner)

My 80s Crossword

Across: 1. Chas 'N' Dave 4. Heaven 7. Out 9. Never 10. SS (Siouxsie Sioux) 11. Heart 12. List 13. ELO (Electric Light Orchestra) 14. Neil 15. Too 16. Radio 17. Down 18. Parr 19. Toto 20. The Kane 22. Joel 24. In 26. NH (Nick Heyward) 28. Give 29. Big Sound 31. Me 33. B.A. 34. On 35. Gang 36. Wah 39. Habit 41. Break 42. You 43. My

Down: 1. Closest Thing To 2. Authority 3. Ain't No Pleasing 4. Here 5. Visions 6. Nasty Girl 8. Hard 10. Slow 15. Tony 21. AC (Aztec Camera) 23. Own 25. One 27. Much 30. SAW (Stock, Aitken, Waterman) 31. Mari 32. Back 37. Day 38. My 39. HM (Helen McCookerybook) 40. To

Monster Mash Up

1. Five Star 2. Only In My Dreams 3. Spandau Ballet 4. 72,000 5. Neil Kinnock 6. Ofra Haza 7. Liverpool 8. Hand In Glove 9. American Gigolo 10. Brothers In Arms by Dire Straits 11. Kids In America by Kim Wilde 12. The Look of Love 13. I Want Your Sex 14. Funky Town 15. 1980 16. Say, Say, Say and The Girl Is Mine 17. London Boys 18. Can't Slow Down 19. Roberta Flack 20. 3 (Johnny Logan 1980, Bucks Fizz 1981, Nicole 1982)

About the author

Born and raised in Kent, Sarah Lewis currently lives in a village near the coastal town of Ramsgate, a return to the countryside in which she grew up. Over the years, her innate interest in music has become a lifelong infatuation with vinyl, radio and gigs. With a desire to share her enthusiasm for the decade of her youth, she has published a number of books, articles and reviews on Eighties' popular culture, appeared on television and radio shows discussing the era, and continues to share its musical delights via her My 80s Radio Show.

Other titles by the author

My Eighties
Your Eighties
More Eighties
The 80's Annual
The 80's Annual, Vol. II

Contact the author

Website: www.my-eighties.com
Blog: myeighties.wordpress.com
Twitter/Facebook: @MyEighties
Instagram: myeighties

#My80s Mixcloud

Mad Wasp Radio